J A

HISTORY

AGUAR

ORY OF A CLASSIC MARQUE

PHILIP PORTER

ORION
BOOKS

A QUINTET BOOK

Published in the United States of America in
1988 by Orion Books, a division of Crown
Publishers Inc., 225 Park Avenue South, New
York, New York 10003 and represented in
Canada by the Canadian MANDA Group

ORION is a trademark of Crown Publishers Inc.

ISBN 0-517-56792-X

This book was designed and produced by
Quintet Publishing Limited
6 Blundell Street
London N7 9BH

Art Director: Peter Bridgewater
Designer: Ian Hunt
Editors: Paul Berman, Robert Stewart,
Shaun Barrington

Typeset in Great Britain by
Central Southern Typesetters, Eastbourne
Manufactured in Hong Kong by Regent
Publishing Services Limited
Printed in Hong Kong by Leefung-Asco Printers
Limited

Library of Congress Cataloging-in-Publication
Data

Porter, Philip
    Jaguar: history of a classic marque.

Includes index.
1. Jaguar automobile — History. 2. Jaguar Cars
British Leyland UK Ltd. — History. I. Title.
TL215, J3P67 1988   629.2'222   87-31269
ISBN 0-517-56792-X

CONTENTS

Foreword 7

From Humble Sidecars 9

A New Name 31

The Exciting XKs 57

The Sporting Sedans 87

The Racing Cats 121

The Sensational XK-E 145

The World Beating XJ Saloons 171

The Legend is Reborn 197

Index 222

ACKNOWLEDGEMENTS AND PICTURE CREDITS

*T*he author and publishers would like to thank Sir John Egan for kindly providing a foreword for this book, and his colleagues in the Communications and Public Affairs department, notably Arnold Bolton and secretaries Bridget and Tracey, for supplying information on recent sales and developments. Thanks are also due to the editors of *Motor, Autocar, The Daily Mail, The Sunday Times* and, of course, to Jaguar Cars Limited for permission to reproduce various images and quotations.

Pictures on pages 218–221 were taken by Andrew Morland. Other illustrations are either from the author's personal collection, or from the Jaguar archives; the very considerable assistance given by Roger Clinkscales of Jaguar Photographic is greatly appreciated.

Finally, the author would like to thank all of those quoted in the book, and the many others interviewed in the last few years, for providing anecdotes, memories, and so much first-hand information.

FOREWORD
BY SIR JOHN EGAN

*I*t is a measure of the very wide interest in the past, present and future of Jaguar that there are so many volumes available on the subject. There is no doubt that the attraction of the marque arises from the beauty of its design and its reputation for performance, culminating in its fabulous victories at Le Mans.

It is these features that have created and fed the enthusiasm of so many people, among them Philip Porter, whose own affection for Jaguar is expressed in several of his published works about the Company and its products.

This book is noteworthy in that it reveals the stories not just of the cars, but of those several stalwarts who have each made a unique contribution to the Company's growth through the years. It provides a captivating history of this classic marque through a galaxy of spectacularly attractive illustrations.

CHAPTER ONE

FROM HUMBLE SIDECARS...

The famous little Austin Seven was the first car to be given the Swallow treatment.

*T*oday Jaguar is one of the most charismatic companies in the world, producing a glamorous range of arguably the finest cars in the world. From its three plants in Coventry and one in Birmingham, in the industrial Midlands, the Jaguar car company manufactures more than 50,000 automobiles, still largely handbuilt, per year. Yet this story began in a small brick garage behind a house in Blackpool, the famous northern seaside town, in 1922.

In that year 20-year-old Billy Lyons met William Walmsley, a man nine years older than him, who had started a small enterprise reconditioning war-surplus Triumph motorcycles and fitting to them a stylish sidecar of his own manufacture. Even at this early age, Lyons demonstrated two of his greatest qualities. He had a brilliant eye for style and an equally brilliant head for business.

Walmsley was content to produce one of his 'combinations' per week, but Lyons shrewdly saw that it was essential for the embryonic enterprise to be organized on a production basis and for output to be considerably increased. Although Walmsley did not share the younger man's enthusiasm and was initially, and perhaps always, a rather reluctant partner, he bowed to family pressure and as soon as Lyons reached his 21st birthday, on 4 September 1922, the two men formed the Swallow Sidecar Company as equal partners, with a bank overdraft of £1,000 from Williams Deacon's Bank (now the Royal Bank of Scotland) guaranteed by their respective fathers.

In fact, some months before Lyons' coming-of-age, premises had been found in Bloomfield Street and a lease taken on the first and second floors of a small industrial building. Several men and a young apprentice were taken on in those early months, when Lyons' father still had to sign company documents on his son's behalf. Advertising began and the young company took a stand at the 1923 Motorcycle Show after one of the participants pulled out at the last minute. Helping to man the Swallow stand was a fellow called Arthur Whittaker, who had joined the company at the age of 17.

The Swallow company prospered in spite of the economic stagnation of the early 1920s. Additional premises were taken at Back Woodfield Road and John Street and then, in 1926, the company was moved to one site, the much larger premises at Cocker Street, and renamed the Swallow Sidecar and Coachbuilding Company. It was there that the venture into car manufacture began.

The Bullnose Morris and, to an even greater extent, the little Austin Seven had dramatically reduced the cost of motoring and were threatening, so it seemed, the future of the motorcycle and sidecar. The occupants of a car also enjoyed protection from the weather. The 'combination' manufacturers were therefore concerned and several of them had started to obtain seven-horsepower chassis from Austin and to clothe them in their own, usually sporting, bodywork. Lyons decided to follow their example. He persuaded Parkers of Bolton and Manchester to sell him a chassis on which to build a prototype. Meanwhile, sidecar sales were still booming and the company's first overseas agent, Emil Frey of Zurich, was appointed.

In early 1927 the Austin Swallow Two-Seater was announced. Constructed of heavy-gauge aluminium over an ash frame and wooden floor, the little Swallow had a distinctive and delightful 'wasp' tail and a detachable hard-top. On early examples the hard-top was hinged (to assist access into this very small car) and the cycle front wings turned with the

WILLIAM LYONS

*W*illiam Lyons was the genius behind Jaguar and it is no exaggeration to say that his life was one of the great success stories of modern times. Born on 4 September 1901 in the northern seaside town of Blackpool, upon leaving school he joined the firm of Crossley Motors as a trainee. He quickly tired of this, however, and returned to Blackpool, where he spent some time in his father's gramophone and piano repair business.

Young Lyons' main passion was for motorcycles and this led, following a brief spell with two garages, Jackson Brothers and Brown & Mallalieu, to his meeting with William Walmsley.

Lyons is remembered as an ambitious man from the earliest days of his enterprise. He combined drive and energy with a shrewd business brain and close attention to costs that some people called meanness. A man who lived for his business, he ploughed his profits back into the company, which came under his sole control when Walmsley left the stage in 1935. He was an autocratic 'boss' who rarely bothered with board meetings and is famous for calling everyone by his surname. Even his later Vice-Chairman was addressed as 'Heynes'! During his lifetime, a number of honours were bestowed upon him, including the Presidency of the Society of Motor Manufacturers, the accolade of Royal Designer to Industry, and a knighthood. Few firms can have exported a greater proportion of their sales, an area spearheaded by Lyons himself, or earned more dollars for Great Britain.

He died in 1985 in his 84th year. He was a brilliant businessman, but perhaps his greatest quality was his eye for style. He understood the importance of style and all his products had it.

wheels (though these gave way almost immediately to fuller, fixed wings). The Austin chassis were used unmodified, apart from the addition of a section of angle iron which ran outside and parallel to the main chassis and on which the body was mounted.

Parkers were appointed selling agents for their area and Brown and Mallalieu looked after Blackpool. With a view to a wider market, Lyons travelled to Birmingham, where he met Stanley Rodway and Norman Steeley, joint Managing Directors of P.J. Evans Limited. To his surprise and pleasure they had no hesitation in ordering 50 cars. Soon after this he arranged a meeting with Frank Hough and Bertie Henly of the thriving London garage business which bore the latter's name. This meeting, the beginning of a long and fruitful relationship, netted an order for no less than 500 Austin Swallows. In return Henly gained sole rights to distribute the cars in southern England.

Towards the end of 1927 Swallow introduced their version of the 1550-cc-engined Morris Cowley chassis. This body, also a two-seater, had a dickey

ARTHUR WHITTAKER

*A*rthur **Whittaker** joined the young Swallow company in the very early days, at the age of 17. Initially involved in sales, he soon moved to assisting Lyons with adminstration and thence to buying, which was to be his forte for many years to come. He became General Manager and, when S.S. Cars went public, a director.

Both William Heynes and Bob Knight feel that Whittaker's role in the Jaguar story has never been sufficiently acknowledged. Heynes remembers him as being a 'very good friend to me'. Both pay tribute to his shrewdness and ability to drive a hard, yet scrupulously fair, bargain. His cute buying of parts at the lowest prices in the industry enabled Lyons to give such remarkable value for money.

In March 1961 his qualities and hard work were recognized by Lyons with the title Deputy Chairman. Seven years later he retired, having given 45 years of loyal service and watched the company grow from a handful of men to an international force.

■ *Motorcycle sidecars were the first products of the Swallow Sidecar Company and Lyons immediately stamped his style on what until then had been somewhat dull and utilitarian additions to the motorcycle.*

EARLY PREMISES

*I*t is most pleasing that the original premises occupied by the fledgling company still survive in largely unchanged form, though they are now somewhat run-down and in 1984 were reported to be up for sale.

The Bloomfield Street building is remarkably small and one can easily see why the extra area at Back Woodfield Road and John Street was needed. The former space was used initially for crating and despatching the sidecars, while the John Street premises were used for storing the bodies and mounting them on to the chassis. The change was of great help to the company, which no longer needed to haul the chassis to the upper floors occupied at Bloomfield Street.

Blackpool is still famous for its trams, but the ones formerly in this area have now gone. The Cocker Street building is also largely unaltered. It is now occupied by a firm of tea and coffee merchants, the proprietor of which lived in the area in the Swallow period. The construction reflects the fact that the building was originally designed to take buses and lorries, and one can still see where the massive lift, which conveyed them to the first floor, once stood.

The local railway station, then known as Talbot Street Station and now named Blackpool North, was conveniently situated just a couple of streets away. From this station the sidecars were despatched and to it the Austin Seven chassis arrived in batches from the Austin works in Birmingham.

In Talbot Square is situated the original branch of Williams Deacon's Bank, which financed the company in its early days and placed its faith in the energetic young man with ambitious plans.

■ *ABOVE With the announcement of the Austin Seven, the popular and economical little car that brought motoring to the masses, the Swallow company graduated to the production of motor cars.*

■ *BELOW Using the Austin Seven chassis as a basis, Swallow produced a very stylish two-seater with an optional hardtop and delightful 'wasp' tail. Interior space was not exactly generous and the hardtop was hinged to ease access.*

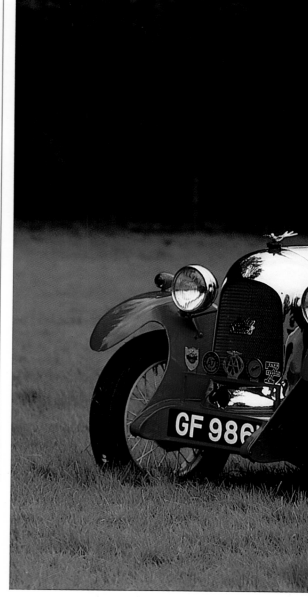

■ *ABOVE AND LEFT At £165 for the model fitted with a 'Cape Hood' and just £5 more for the 'de Luxe' version, the brightly painted Austin Swallow Sports Two-Seaters offered remarkable value allied to distinctively individual good looks.*

■ *BELOW The larger Morris Cowley chassis received the Swallow treatment, but very few were made; the company prospered as demand remained strong for the little Austin.*

(or rumble) seat in the sloping tail. It sold for £220 with wire wheels, £10 less without. Very little is known about this model and very few were made.

Meanwhile it was chaos at Cocker Street. Swallow was outgrowing even those premises. There was a desperate lack of storage space and a bottleneck in the varnishing shop, where only two cars could be processed per day. The Henly order dictated another move and this time a more radical one. The centre of the motor industry was in the Midlands, around Coventry and Birmingham, where most of Swallow's suppliers were situated and where there was a pool of skilled labour. Being in Blackpool meant that the company had to absorb heavy carriage costs, both for chassis and for components. Furthermore it was not easy to obtain the skilled men required and Swallow had already resorted to advertising in Midlands newspapers. In 1928 premises were therefore found on the Whitmore Park estate in the Foleshill district of Coventry and the move was made to this old and run-

down former munitions factory just off Holbrook Lane. Just before the move, the Austin Two-Seater had been supplemented by the introduction of a saloon body on the same Austin Seven chassis and the 'new' factory allowed production to be increased to 50 cars per week. The sidecars were still proving popular, but although their steady sales confounded forecasts and provided useful stability, they were to play a less and less important role as time went by.

One of the things that made the Swallows stand out in a crowd was their adventurous, one might even say loud, paint schemes. In an age when most cars wore sombre blacks and dark browns and greens, the little Swallows were bright and bold. The Morris was finished in 'cream and crimson lake' with red leather upholstery. No wonder the cars were noticed! The Austins

were no exception. They included such delightful choices as 'Sky Blue and Danish Blue' and 'Light Mole Brown and Deep Suede Brown'. The saloon bodywork was of similar construction to the open car and the wooden-framed roof had a distinctive peak, rather like a peaked cap.

The paint scheme is often referred to as a 'pen-nib' effect because the upper colour which was applied to the body above the waistline came to a point at the radiator cowl. These small luxury saloons were very well finished and included such niceties as a lady's companion set by Houbigant. And since they were reliable, inexpensive and relatively easy to drive, it is not surprising that a good proportion of the Swallows found favour with the ladies.

A larger vehicle was needed to complement the Austins and in 1929 the

■ *A more practical version of the Austin Swallow supplemented the Two-Seater with the introduction of the Austin Swallow Saloon, a family car with four somewhat cramped seats. The model was a great success and its sales, together with the ever-increasing production of sidecars, dictated a radical expansion of the company and a move to the Midlands, traditional heart of the motor industry.*

■ *ABOVE It was never officially stated whether the initials 'S.S.', the name by which all the new models were henceforth to be known, stood for 'Standard Swallow', 'Swallow Sidecar' or even, as has been suggested, 'Super Sports'.*

■ *BELOW The association between the established Standard Motor Co. and Swallow proved to be a most fruitful one for Swallow. The relationship began with the building of Swallow bodies on the 9hp and 15hp Standard chassis.*

company, which a year earlier had built a one-off body on an Alvis, obtained a batch of obsolete FIAT 509A chassis. Sir Herbert Austin had treated Lyons with less than courtesy and the 'coming man' was always keen to find alternative chassis for the familiar treatment. Between 50 and 100 FIAT Swallows were produced.

The range was joined on the 1929 Motor Show stand by Swallow coachwork on the Swift Ten and, more significantly, the Standard Big Nine. The Swift, based on the 1190-cc-engined 'Fleetwing' chassis, was produced during 1930 and 1931. The Standard was of greater significance because it marked the commencement of a long and fruitful relationship. The Big Nine, which in Swallow form was priced at £245, was most fashionable, with its long bonnet and low roofline suggesting rather more in the way of performance than it actually delivered.

By now production was in the region of 100 cars per week and the range was again supplemented by the addition of a larger 15-hp six-cylinder-engined Standard Ensign Swallow. Just over 50 models were made, which served to introduce the firm to Standard's excellent, smooth 2054-cc side-valve power unit. The Standard company and this particular engine were to feature in Lyons' and Walmsley's plans, for they were tiring of designing bodies to suit borrowed chassis and yearned for the freedom of having chassis to their own design and specification. That was the next step.

Meanwhile Lyons designed another quite delightful body on the Wolseley Hornet chassis, offered to the public first in two-seater form and later as a four-seater as well. The first model was launched in 1930 and the two versions continued until 1932. In the same year Wolseley introduced the four-speed, twin-carburettor Hornet Special, which received the same two variations of bodywork until these models, the last Swallows, were dropped in 1933.

In 1931 the sensational S.S.'s were launched. With a new chassis specially designed and exclusively produced by Standard for Swallow, Lyons was able to design an extraordinarily low and dramatic body. As the adverts stated, these new cars had 'the £1000 look', yet cost a modest £310. By mounting the road springs alongside the chassis rather than below, as was the contemporary practice, Lyons achieved an exceptionally low line. Indeed it

THE AUTOCAR.

JULY 31ST. 1931.

WAIT!
THE *SS* IS COMING
2 New Coupés of Surpassing Beauty

● S.S. is the new name of a new car that's going to thrill the hearts of the motoring public and the trade alike. It's something utterly new...different...better!

Long...low...very low...and very FAST! At the Show, or before, two S.S. Coupés of surpassing beauty will be presented. WAIT...THE S.S. IS COMING

AND THE EXTREMELY SUCCESSFUL STANDARD SWALLOW 4-SEATER SALOONS TO BE CONTINUED

BIG NINE FULL 4-STR. SALOON, £250.   15 h.p. 6-cyl. full 4-seater Saloon, £275.

SWALLOW
EXCLUSIVE COACHWORK

SWALLOW COACHBUILDING COMPANY, FOLESHILL, COVENTRY.
London Showrooms : Henly House, Euston Road, N.W.1.   Telephone : Coventry 8027.
Agents throughout the country.

EMIL FREY

Whether the appointment of Emil Frey was an act of inspiration or pure luck it is hard to say. Certainly it turned out to be a masterly move.

Lyons and Frey met on the Swallow stand at the 1926 Olympia Show and shook hands on an agreement whereby Frey was given the exclusive dealership for Switzerland and, by ordering 20 sidecars there and then, the rights to a similar selling arrangement for future products of the Swallow company. Like Lyons, Frey started in a small way and through hard work and ability built a large empire. Like Lyons, he was a motorcycle enthusiast who loved to race motorcycles and sidecars. In this way he promoted the Swallow name in his native country to good effect. When Lyons moved on to the manufacture of cars, Frey sold them and laid the foundations of his multi-million-pound garage business. In the early 1980s when Jaguar, still under the BL umbrella, wished to form its own company in Germany, it wisely took the Frey Group as its partner.

The partnership which William Lyons and Emil Frey started all those years ago celebrated 60 years of mutual success in 1986 and is continued today by Sir John Egan and Emil's son, Walter, the company's Chief Executive since 1969.

■ TOP LEFT *Swallow advertising was always as bold as its colour schemes and in July, 1931, an aura of style and distinction was already being created around the new cars.*

■ LEFT *The Swallow body on a Wolseley Hornet chassis, seen here in two-seater form, was particularly attractive and the nearest approach yet to a genuine sports car.*

was stated that two short men could easily shake hands over the roof or peer in through the open sliding roof! The engine was mounted well back in the frame and the bonnet was outrageously long. The initials 'S.S.' were coined to identify the new cars, though it was never stated whether they stood for Standard Swallow, Swallow Sports or Swallow Sidecars.

The S.S.I was fitted with Standard's 16-hp 2054-cc engine and supplemented, a little later, by the same company's 20-hp side-valve 2552-cc unit. Performance was fair. It certainly did not live up to the aura created by the excessively sporting style, but roadholding, owing to the low centre of gravity, was good for the period. Alongside the S.S.I was offered a smaller-bodied version, fitted to Standard's Little Nine chassis with a four-cylinder 1006-cc power unit. The body was a scaled-down version of the larger car and looked good, which is more than can be said for its very modest performance. The price of £210 was, however, most competitive.

The early S.S.'s had been rather hurriedly designed and built in order to make their debut at the 1931 Olympia Show. Lyons had been ill just before the Show, moreover, and was not able to exercise complete control over their final shape. Consequently the company's transition to more complete motor manufacturing was a traumatic one, with many teething problems experienced by early owners.

For the 1932 Show the larger model was considerably revised and improved. The wheelbase was lengthened by seven inches and the track by two, enabling the rear seats to be occupied by adults. To create even more

---

♦ S.S.I COUPE ♦
1ST SERIES

BODY STYLE(s): Fixed Head Coupe
ENGINE: Side-valve 6 cyl, 2054 & 2552 cc
MAX POWER: 45 bhp & 55 bhp
TIME: 0–50 20 secs (2054 cc)
MAX SPEED: 70 mph
QUANTITY MADE: 502
PRICE: £310 & £320
ANNOUNCEMENT DATE: Oct 1931
IN PRODUCTION: 1932

■ *To many people the new S.S.I was an outlandish car, with an outrageous and expensive style that was not matched by its performance; the price, however, was modest. The dickey, or rumble, seat was not a standard feature.*

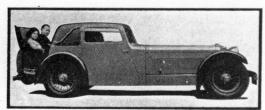

■ *RIGHT AND BELOW The chassis of the S.S.I Coupe was built exclusively for the Swallow company, allowing Lyons a freer hand to design the body. The body was, for the period, incredibly low-slung, with the rear seats 'split' by the prop shaft. The view from behind the wheel was of an excessively long bonnet.*

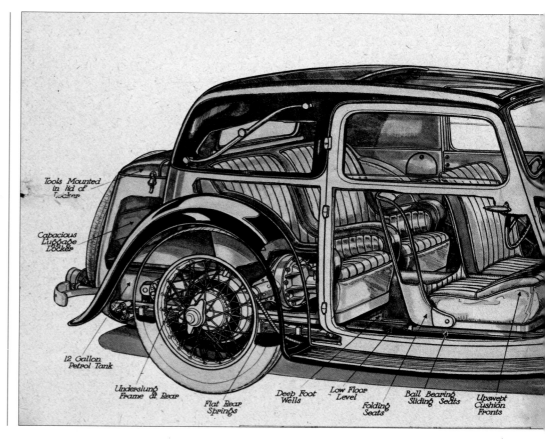

Tools Mounted in lid of Locker

Capacious Luggage Locker

12 Gallon Petrol Tank

Underslung Frame at Rear

Flat Rear Springs

Deep Foot Wells

Low Floor Level

Folding Seats

Ball Bearing Sliding Seats

Upswept Cushion Fronts

■ *BOTTOM The little S.S.II was overshadowed by its larger sister, but, based on the Standard Little Nine chassis, it offered remarkable value and sold well.*

♦ S.S. II COUPE ♦

1ST SERIES

BODY STYLE(s): Fixed Head Coupe
ENGINE: Side-valve 4 cyl, 1006 cc
MAX POWER: 28 bhp
TIME: 0–50 26.6 secs
MAX SPEED: 60 mph
QUANTITY MADE: 549
PRICE: £210
ANNOUNCEMENT DATE: Oct 1931
IN PRODUCTION: 1932–1933

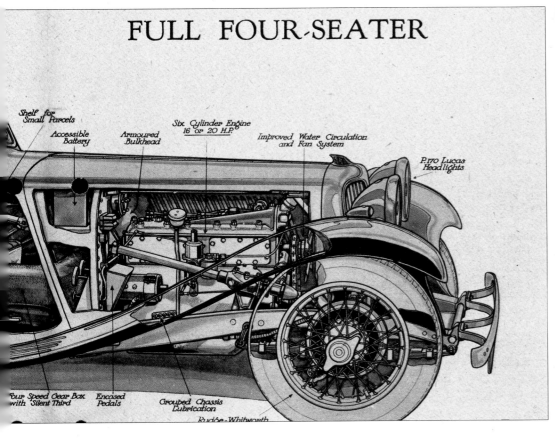

FULL FOUR-SEATER

Shelf for Small Parcels

Accessible Battery

Armoured Bulkhead

Six Cylinder Engine 16 or 20 H.P

Improved Water Circulation and Fan System

P.170 Lucas Head lights

Four Speed Gear Box with Silent Third

Encased Pedals

Grouped Chassis Lubrication

Rudge-Whitworth

┌─────────────────────────────┐

♦ S.S.I COUPE ♦

2ND SERIES

BODY STYLE(s): Fixed Head Coupe
ENGINE: Side-valve 6 cyl,
  2054 & 2552 cc (1933)
  2143 & 2663 cc (1934)
MAX POWER: 48 bhp & 62 bhp (1933)
  53 bhp & 68 bhp (1934)
  62 bhp & 70 bhp (1935)
TIME: 0–50 28.4 secs & 21.4 secs (1933)
MAX SPEED: 75 mph & 81.8 mph (1933)
QUANTITY MADE: 1099 (1933) 200 (1934/5)
PRICE: £325 (1933) £335 (1934/5)
ANNOUNCEMENT DATE: Sept 1932
IN PRODUCTION: 1933–1936

└─────────────────────────────┘

■ *BELOW The early S.S.I's were somewhat impractical, but like the smaller cars they benefited from gradual development and refinement, without losing the essential style and value for money which were the Swallow Company's hallmark.*

rear legroom, the chassis was underslung at the rear. The individual front wings were superseded by the more usual type which flowed to the rear ones. The S.S.II remained largely unchanged apart from the adoption of a four-speed gearbox.

In spite of the difficult economic times, these models sold well and production of the S.S.I doubled to approximately 1100 in 1933. The fact that the S.S.'s looked expensive allowed people who had previously owned, say, Bentleys to keep up appearances. In the same year the Tourer, an open four-seater model, was introduced and some 150 were sold. Towards the end of the year another model joined the range. The Saloon, with its more conventional pairs of side windows, was a more practical rendering of the same basic style and allowed the rear seat passengers the luxury of a view of the outside world.

Alongside the introduction of the Saloon, all the S.S.I's were offered with enlarged 2143-cc or 2663 engines and the track was again increased by two inches. At the same time the smallest S.S.II's were considerably improved. A new specially-designed chassis was adopted with an 8 ft 8 in wheelbase, 14½ in longer than before and the previous 3 ft 9 in track was extended by 1½ in. This, together with the adoption of 1343 and 1608-cc engines and the introduction of a Saloon model, considerably improved the model's appeal.

The more practical Saloon now outsold the Coupe versions by five-and-a-half to one. The Tourers did well and in 1934 the S.S.II was offered in this form. In the same year, the Airline Saloon was added to the larger range. Lyons was following the vogue for this particular style of coachwork, and though he never liked the car himself, it was widely praised and more than 600 models were sold in the years it was offered, 1935 and 1936.

Competitive events in this period normally took the form of 'concours d'élégance' rather than competitive motoring. There were exceptions, however, and S.S.'s ventured into events such as rallies with increasing frequency. Experience rather than results was gained by a team of three S.S.I Tourers at the International Alpine Trial of 1933. However, they

■ ABOVE For 1934 the S.S.II Coupe gained its own, specially designed chassis; it was significantly lengthened, making the car more habitable.

■ RIGHT The S.S.I Tourer was a pleasant and logical addition to the range.

◆ S.S.I TOURER ◆

BODY STYLE(s): Open Four Seater
ENGINE: Side-valve 6 cyl,
  2054 & 2552 cc (1933)
  2143 & 2663 cc (1934)
MAX POWER: 48 bhp & 62 bhp (1933)
  53 bhp & 68 bhp (1934)
  62 bhp & 70 bhp (1935)
TIME: 0–50 23 secs (1935 2663 cc)
QUANTITY MADE: 551
PRICE: £325 (2054 cc)   £335 (2552 cc)
  £335 (2143 cc)   £340 (2663 cc)
ANNOUNCEMENT DATE: March 1933 &
  Oct 1933
IN PRODUCTION: 1933–1934 & 1934–1936

The *new* S.S. OPEN FOUR-SEATER SPORTS

This intriguing full four-seater Sports offers performance and luxury usually found only in cars double the price. It appeals not only to the sportsman but to the man who considers comfort. The high efficiency engine ensures fast maximum and cruising speeds with exceptional acceleration. Efficient all-weather protection is provided and in every detail the car meets the most exacting requirements of the discerning motorist. Call and arrange a trial run and at the same time obtain details of our exchange and convenient purchase terms.

2 - LITRE
16 H.P. S. S. 1
£325

2½ - LITRE
20 H.P. S. S. 1
£335

BIRMINGHAM DISTRIBUTORS:

P.J. EVANS L^{TD}
RODWAY & STEELEY
JOHN BRIGHT ST. BIRMINGHAM
Telephone: Midland 2910.   Telegrams: "Lytcar, B'ham."

CONSTANCE TEATHER REMEMBERS THE EARLY DAYS

Young Connie Dickson left school at 16½ and, after working for a short while for a company until it closed down, saw an advertisement for a secretarial job at Swallow in April 1928. A large number of girls had already attended for an interview on the Saturday morning when Connie, who had not seen the advert immediately, went along on the Monday.

'After waiting a little while, I was shown into Mr. Lyons' office and he gave me a test of my shorthand and percentages and decimals. Then we talked about wages and I was offered five shillings a week. So I said, "Oh no, I can't manage with five shillings because it costs me more than that to come on the train". So then he offered me ten shillings a week and I agreed because I was very anxious to work.

'In a corner of the Stores there was a small office built and that's where Mr. Whittaker was installed and I was his typist. We did all the buying and service queries. I was also told to give the nuts and bolts out to the men as they needed them but I said, "No, I'm a shorthand typist and I don't think I should do that!" So instead they brought Harry Teather, who had joined the company in 1923, up to look after the stores.

'I got to know Alice Fenton, who had already joined the company, very well and we became very good friends. It was a great shock to me when a notice went up to say that they'd decided to move to Coventry.'

Following the move to Coventry, Alice Fenton (who years later was to become Home Sales Director) persuaded her friend Connie to move there. Connie later married Harry Teather who retired in 1973 as Executive Director, Purchasing.

Capt. G.E.T. EYSTON

THE HON. BRIAN LEWIS

Mr. JOHN COBB

3 *famous experts enthusiastic about*
S.S. PERFORMANCE

Capt. G. E. T. EYSTON says: "It... has a sparkling performance which includes excellent steering and braking... The comfort and ease of handling under all conditions is a delight."

The Hon. BRIAN LEWIS says: "I was really astonished at the performance of this car... Its maximum speed is all that one could desire, and the easy cruising speed... high above the average..."

Mr. JOHN COBB says: "I am amazed at the wonderful performance of the S.S. Its acceleration, its roadholding, its maintenance of high speeds without effort, and its powerful brakes, compel my admiration."

(Extracts from letters received from these famous racing drivers)

You, too, will be enthusiastic about the S.S. after a trial run. Get in touch with us to-day. Art catalogue on request. S.S.1. prices from £335. S.S.11. prices from £260.

HENLYS S.S. DISTRIBUTORS FOR SOUTHERN ENGLAND & MANCHESTER. Devonshire House, Piccadilly, W.1. Henly House, Euston Road, N.W.1. (Museum 7734) and at Manchester & Bournemouth.

S.S.1 4-Seater Saloon £340

Manufacturers: S.S. Cars Ltd., Holbrook Lane, Coventry.

♦ S.S.I SALOON ♦

BODY STYLE(s): Four-light Saloon (four side windows)
ENGINE: Side-valve 6 cyl, 2143 & 2663 cc
MAX POWER: 53 bhp & 68 bhp (1934) 62 bhp & 70 bhp (1935)
TIME: 0–60 24 secs (1935 2663 cc)
MAX SPEED: 81.5 mph (1935 2663 cc)
QUANTITY MADE: 1144
PRICE: £340 & £345
ANNOUNCEMENT DATE: Oct 1933
IN PRODUCTION: 1933–1936

■ *LEFT AND FAR LEFT The S.S.I Coupe sacrificed some comforts to style (the rear seats, for example, were not places for people with a tendency to claustrophobia). The S.S.I Saloon was a more practical alternative. It was, in the phraseology of the period, a 'four light saloon', having four side windows and allowing the rear seat passengers more pleasant accommodation.*

■ *BELOW The smaller S.S.II Coupe received the same treatment as the S.S.I and was offered as a saloon. When fitted with the 10hp Standard engine, this model cost just £235; 12hp was available for a further £5!*

♦ S.S.II COUPE ♦
SALOON, TOURER
2ND SERIES

BODY STYLE(s): Fixed Head Coupe, Four-light Saloon, Open Four Seater
ENGINE: Side-valve 4 cyl, 1343 & 1608 cc
MAX POWER: 32 bhp & 38 bhp
TIME: Not Available
MAX SPEED: 61.2 mph
QUANTITY MADE: Coupe 154   Saloon 905   Tourer 186
PRICE: Not Available
ANNOUNCEMENT DATE: Coupe & Saloon Oct 1933 Tourer March 1934
IN PRODUCTION: Coupe & Saloon 1934–1936 Tourer 1934–1935

returned the following year and collected the team award.

Lyons, as ever, was ambitious and keen to expand whereas Walmsley was a reluctant partner. In November 1934 the partnership was dissolved when Walmsley resigned. In January of the following year S.S. Cars became a public company and Lyons was made Chairman and Managing Director.

Two months later two more models – the S.S.I Drophead and the S.S. 90 – were added to the growing Swallow range. The Drophead was a most stylish variation on the S.S.I theme, with a folding hood which disappeared completely from view under a hinged tonneau panel behind the seats. It closely resembled the Coupe, with its folding 'wig top' and operating 'pram irons'. As the entire S.S.I range was soon to be replaced, hardly more than 100 Dropheads were made. They were sold at the very reasonable price of £380 for the 16-hp model and £385 for the 20-hp version. The other new model was even more exciting. The S.S.90, fitted with a 20-hp 2,663-cc side-valve engine, was the company's first genuine sports car. It did not have a particularly inspiring performance, in spite of engine development by the renowned expert, Harry Weslake, but its scintillating good looks were a foretaste of things to come.

The S.S.'s had managed to capture a market on looks alone; but it was necessary, if business stability and progress were to be maintained, for Lyons to add engineering merit to the formula.

♦ S.S.I AIRLINE ♦

BODY STYLE: Fastback Saloon
ENGINE: Side-valve 6 cyl, 2143 & 2663 cc
MAX POWER: 62 bhp & 70 bhp
TIME: Not Available
MAX SPEED: 80 mph
QUANTITY MADE: 624
PRICE: £360 & £365
ANNOUNCEMENT DATE: Sept 1934
IN PRODUCTION: 1935–1936

■ *ABOVE, LEFT AND FAR LEFT* The S.S.I Airline was something of an anomaly, but it catered for a fashion for this style of body – perhaps the first and last time that Lyons allowed himself to be swayed by fashion. The Airline was not a personal favourite of his, but the sales figures showed that it was popular with a number of customers.

■ *TOP FAR LEFT* For those consumers who could not afford the S.S.I Tourer or preferred a smaller car, the S.S.II was offered as an open four-seater tourer.

♦THE S.S.I DROPHEAD COUPE♦

ENGINE: Specially manufactured Standard six cylinder. 16 hp; 65.5 m/m bore × 106 m/m stroke; 2143 cc 20 hp; 73 m/m bore × 106 m/m stroke; 2663.7 cc. Side by side valves. Exceptionally stiff seven-bearing crankshaft, 2¼″ diameter main bearings. 1¾″ diameter big ends. Aluminium pistons. Chromium iron cylinder blocks. Light alloy connecting rods. Machined combustion chambers and ports. Two special high-speed R.A.G. carburettors. High efficiency induction and exhaust manifold. Detachable high compression aluminium cylinder head. Cooling by centrifugal pump and fan with adjustable thermostat. High pressure submerged oil pump. Coil ignition. Single dry plate light action clutch.

FRAME: Low underslung frame designed for extreme rigidity. The main members are triangulated in the centre by cross bracing from the dumb irons to the rear spring brackets.

TRANSMISSION: Synchro-mesh gears on second, third and top. Hardy-Spicer all-metal propeller shaft and universal joints. Spiral bevel final drive. Easy to hand change speed lever.

GEAR RATIOS: 16 hp: Top, 4.50; Third, 6.18; Second, 9.51; First, 16.20. 20 hp: Top 4.25; Third, 5.83; Second, 8.98; First, 15.30.

SUSPENSION: Ensuring smooth and steady road-holding with maximum comfort at all speeds. Long flat road springs of low periodicity, mounted on "Silentbloc" bushes. The easily accessible jacking pads ensure quick erection. Hartford friction type shock absorbers front and rear.

BRAKES: Highly efficient Bendix Duo-Servo. Hand and foot operated on all four wheels. Quick-action spring release hand brake lever of racing type.

STEERING: Marles Weller cam and lever type.

AXLES: Semi-floating rear axle with one-piece steel casing. Four pinion differential. Front axle: "H" section with reversed Elliott stub axles.

PETROL SUPPLY: By A.C. pump with auxiliary priming lever for hand operation, from 12 gallon tank at the rear of the chassis. The tank filler is of 2½″ diameter with quickly detachable bayonet fixing cap.

WHEELS AND TYRES: Rudge-Whitworth centre-lock splined hub type racing wheels. 18″ rims with chromium plated rim edges fitted with Dunlop 5.50 × 18 tyres. Spare wheel with metal cover cellulosed to match car.

ELECTRICAL EQUIPMENT: 12-volt set. Large type QED 166S, GC headlamps with motif to match radiator cap, and dip and switch control above steering wheel. Finger-tip operated ignition control. Stop light. Reversing light. Sports type wing lamps. Special Lucas type blended note horns, domed to match head lamps, chromium plated with grille fronts to match the radiator, are fitted to each dumb iron. Lamps and horns all chromium plated finish.

COACHWORK: The body, constructed on the soundest lines, is of extreme strength. The frame is of prime quality selected ash throughout, reinforced by aluminium and steel brackets.

DOORS: Flush fitting and exceptionally wide, ensuring ease of access.

WINDSCREEN: Patent type of simplified design, with swept top rail, and radiused corners. Opens from the bottom and is quickly operated. Concealed hinges, obviating any obstruction of vision. Lucas duo-blade windscreen wiper.

WINDOWS: Saloon type, winding windows with chromium-plated metal frames. May be adjusted to any position whether head is up or down.

CANTRAIL-PILLARS: An exclusive SS feature, the cantrail-pillars are instantly detachable and are carried in special compartments in the doors. If preferred, the cantrail-pillars may be left in position when the head is lowered.

HEAD: Of the finest quality proofed fabric. Head-sticks chromium plated and bound with material to match head. Rear light with chromium plated frame. Heavily chromium plated head joints.

TRUNK: All-metal, with chromium-plated security catches and lock. Constructed to contain and totally conceal the hood; also provides accommodation for luggage. Tools are housed in a special compartment on the underside of the lid.

BONNET: Stainless steel hinge, and heavily louvred side panels with quick action security fasteners.

WINGS: One-piece pressings, with deep valances, ensuring adequate protection.

UPHOLSTERY: Finest quality Vaumol hide throughout, in a range of colours to tone with the exterior colour scheme.

CABINET WORK: Instrument panel, door cappings and fillets are of polished figured walnut finish.

CARPETING: The floor is thickly carpeted in colours to harmonise with the exterior finish.

SEATS: Four adult passengers are accommodated in the highest degree of comfort. The rear seats are constructed as two small armchairs, deeply sprung with Swallow patent spring case cushions and back rests. The arm rest is heavily padded with a special cushion rubber. (The arm rest may be omitted if desired, but the axle shaft tunnel renders a one-piece cushion impracticable.) Deep foot wells provide ample leg room. The front seats are constructed on similar lines to those at the rear, but there is, of course, no arm rest. The front seats are quickly adjustable by means of special slide rails, whilst the back rests hinge forward.

HEAD ROOM: Sufficient for the tallest passenger is made possible by the special dropped chassis frame.

INSTRUMENTS: Illuminated panel with hexagon mountings for electric clock, 100 mph trip speedometer with revolution markings, ammeter, oil pressure gauge and radiator thermometer combined, and electric petrol gauge.

DIMENSIONS: Wheelbase, 9′ 11″. Track, 4′ 5⅜″. Overall length, 15′ 6″. Overall width, 5′ 5½″. Overall height, 4′ 7″. Width of body inside, 4′ 0″. Width of doors, 3′ 6″. Centre of backrest to pedals (adjustable), 3′ 8″ maximum; 3′ 2″ minimum. Height of backrest (front and rear), 2′ 1″. Depth of body inside, 3′ 5″. Back of front seat to centre of rear seat backrest, 3′ 6″ maximum; 3′ 1″ minimum.

EARLY EXPORTS

During the S.S. era, the company established agencies throughout Europe with garages in France, Austria, Portugal, Spain, Sweden, Holland, Czechoslovakia, Belgium and, of course, Switzerland. Similar deals were struck in Egypt, India, Palestine, Australia and Morocco and cars were also supplied to Madeira, Jamaica and Poland. In the United States, S.S.'s were handled by British Motors in New York County, where the salesman was no less a personage than His Royal Highness, Prince of the Asturias.

■ LEFT Swallow advertising was never self-effacing and this technical description taken from the S.S.I brochure is no exception.

♦S.S.I DROPHEAD♦ COUPE

BODY STYLE: Similar in appearance to Coupe, but with folding top
ENGINE: Side-valve 6 cyl, 2143 & 2663 cc
MAX POWER: 62 bhp & 70 bhp
TIME: Not Available
MAX SPEED: 80 mph
QUANTITY MADE: 100
PRICE: £380 & £385
ANNOUNCEMENT DATE: March 1935
IN PRODUCTION: 1935–1936

■ *ABOVE* The S.S.I Tourers were the first Swallow cars to be used to good effect in competition work. Shown here is a model competing in an International Alpine Trial.

♦ S . S . 9 0 ♦

BODY STYLE: Two Seater Sports
ENGINE: Side-valve 6 cyl, 2663 cc
MAX POWER: 70 bhp
TIME: 0–60 17 secs
MAX SPEED: 90 mph
QUANTITY MADE: 24
PRICE: £395
ANNOUNCEMENT DATE: March 1935
IN PRODUCTION: 1935–1936 (only one made in 1936)

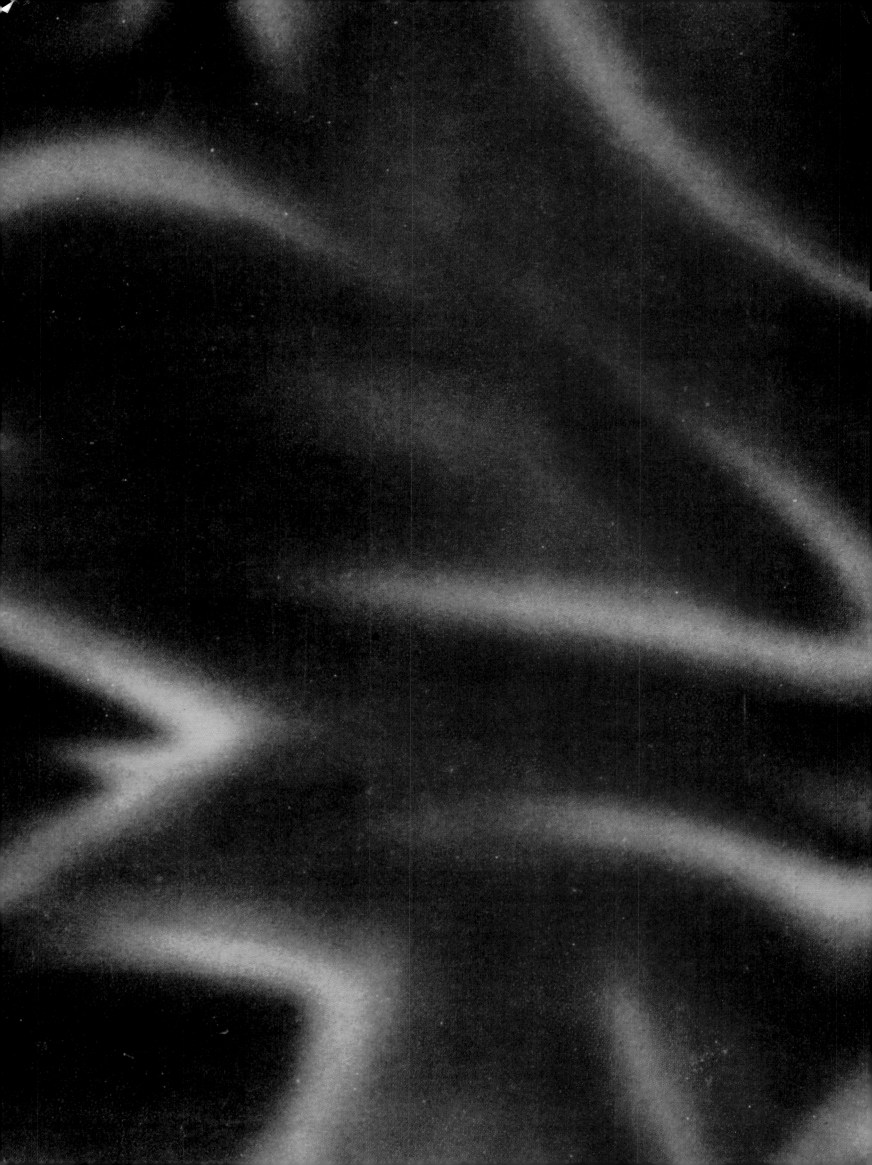

CHAPTER TWO

A NEW NAME

*In 1935 the name of Jaguar was added to
SS, and with it came a greater technical
integrity and sophistication.*

*L*yons addressed himself to the need to give his stylish machines more credibility by appointing a young man called William Heynes as his Chief Engineer in April 1935. It was another stroke of genius, for Heynes was to play a part in this story second only to that of his employer.

Heynes' immediate tasks were to set up an engineering department and design a new chassis for a completely new range which Lyons intended to announce in the autumn. The company was becoming more sophisticated and the new products reflected that. The new range was given the name Jaguar and henceforward all models were to be known as SS Jaguars.

The new saloons were conservative in looks yet still had a tremendous style – distinctly reminiscent of certain Bentleys – at a fraction of the price. They continued to foster Lyons' growing reputation for offering value for money that his competitors could not match.

Arthur Whittaker, who joined the board as General Manager when the company went public, was responsible for buying. He was a tough negotiator with suppliers and his astute buying considerably aided Lyons' ability to sell his cars so cheaply. Indeed, the story is told that Whittaker would go by the weight of a component. He would look at it, weigh it, consider the number of components and then inform the supplier of a fair price!

To give the SS cars the performance they required, Lyons hired Harry Weslake, who was making a name for himself as an independent consultant specializing in cylinder-head work, to raise the Standard engine's power output. Weslake decided to convert the 2½-litre engine to overhead valve operation. So successful was the new design that output increased from 75 hp to 105 hp, comfortably exceeding the 95 hp stipulated in Weslake's contract.

The new bodies continued to be coachbuilt with steel panels (the manufacture of which was sub-contracted out) over an ash frame in the traditional manner. However, the new car was the first from the marque to have four doors. The radiator grille was a new and particularly imposing design. Heynes widened the S.S.I chassis and increased its rigidity. A wider body was made possible by mounting the rear springs inside the chassis and Girling brakes were adopted.

Announced at the same 1935 Show was the 1½-litre version of the new SS Jaguar saloon. This shared the new improved chassis, though in shortened form, and the same high standard of luxury and fittings, but

Models and Prices: Jaguar 2½ Litre Saloon (illustrated above) £385. Jaguar 2½ Litre Open Tourer, £375. Jaguar 2½ Litre "100" Competition Model, £395. Jaguar 1½ Litre Saloon, £295.

◆ S S J A G U A R ◆
2 ½ LITRE SALOON & TOURER

BODY STYLE(s): Two Door, Four Seater
Saloon & Open Four Seater
ENGINE: Overhead valve 6 cyl 2663 cc
MAX POWER: 102 bhp
TIME: 0–60 17.4 secs
MAX SPEED: 85.7 mph
QUANTITY MADE: Saloon 3413 Tourer 98
PRICE: Saloon £385 Tourer £375
ANNOUNCEMENT DATE: Sept 1935
IN PRODUCTION: 1936–1937

■ *The models in the new SS Jaguar range had greater technical integrity and were less outwardly flamboyant than their predecessors, reflecting a growing sophistication in the company's products. Company policy, extremely successful, was to offer the style of the most prestigious cars at a fraction of their cost.*

WILLIAM HEYNES

Bill Heynes is perhaps the second most important figure, after Sir William Lyons, in the Jaguar story. A naturally gifted engineer, he built a team that was second to none in the British post-war motor industry.

Born in 1903, he served his apprenticeship at Humber, where he won respect and promotion. When Lyons decided he needed a chief engineer, Heynes was recommended by his former bosses, who now worked for Standard and with whom Lyons had close contact. It was one of Lyons' finest decisions. Heynes' task was formidable, but in a short space of time he succeeded in designing a new chassis and making sundry improvements so that the new SS Jaguars could be announced in late 1935. From that time onwards every Jaguar designed was the work of Bill Heynes or the gradually expanding team working under him.

He considerably improved the chassis designs, which culminated in the superbly strong XK and the large saloon chassis. He masterminded the XK engine design and the unitary-construction small saloons. The E-type he designed in conjunction with Malcolm Sayer.

Always a racing enthusiast, he conceived the C-types and D-types that took on and beat the best over 24 hours. He would have liked to continue racing if he could have persuaded Lyons; and he did later build the mid-engined XJ13 which so sadly was never developed or raced.

Jaguars justifiably have a reputation for style and value for money. Bill Heynes ensured that they had a reputation for performance as well and he pioneered many engineering achievements that we take for granted today.

♦ S S J A G U A R ♦
1 ½ LITRE SALOON

BODY STYLE: Two Door, Four Seater Saloon
ENGINE: Side-valve 4 cyl, 1608 cc
MAX POWER: 52 bhp
TIME: 0–60 33 secs
MAX SPEED: 70 mph
QUANTITY MADE: 2208
PRICE: £285
ANNOUNCEMENT DATE: Sept 1936
IN PRODUCTION: 1936–1938

■ *ABOVE The new Jaguars were offered with 1½-litre (seen here) and 2½-litre engines. The saloons benefited from a chassis redesigned by the new chief engineer, William Heynes, and now had four doors. The 2½-litre engines were modified to overhead valve operation by Harry Weslake, the distinguished engine consultant.*

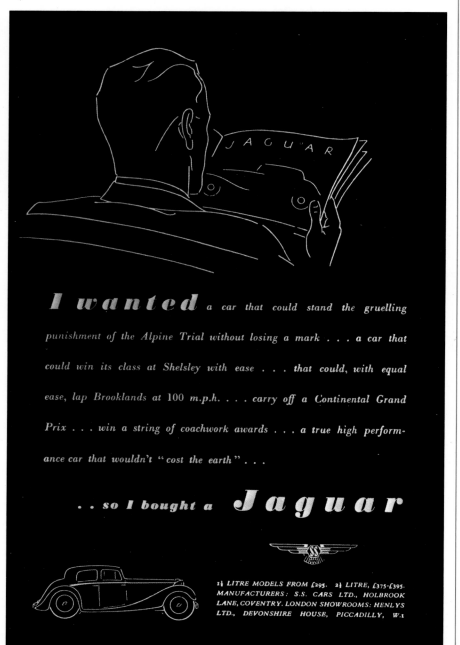

I wanted a car that could stand the gruelling punishment of the Alpine Trial without losing a mark . . . a car that could win its class at Shelsley with ease . . . that could, with equal ease, lap Brooklands at 100 m.p.h. . . . carry off a Continental Grand Prix . . . win a string of coachwork awards . . . a true high perform- ance car that wouldn't "cost the earth" . . .

. . so I bought a Jaguar

1¼ LITRE MODELS FROM £295. 2¼ LITRE, £375-£395. MANUFACTURERS: S.S. CARS LTD., HOLBROOK LANE, COVENTRY. LONDON SHOWROOMS: HENLYS LTD., DEVONSHIRE HOUSE, PICCADILLY, W.1

■ *RIGHT SS advertising employed a certain amount of licence and of course no single model really achieved all this; but it certainly looks highly impressive.*

ERNEST 'BILL' RANKIN

Bill Rankin played a vital but usually overlooked role in the development of the company. Following a period as an advertising representative for General Motors after World War I and after winning a competition for an advertising and promotion scheme for the Watney Brewery, for whom he created the famous 'Red Barrel', he joined Jaguar Cars.

As advertising manager, he was involved with the choice of the Jaguar name, the designing of the leaping Jaguar and the building of the Jaguar aura. His successor, Bob Berry, who worked with him after 1951, comments that before he joined the company, 'it was very much a one man band. Really if it was written, printed or advertised, Rankin was responsible for it.' Lyons had many ideas but it was Rankin who translated them into advertisements. Working closely with the Nelson Advertising Agency, he made an important, yet unquantifiable, contribution to Jaguar sales. Following his death in 1966, the late Eric Brown, former Chairman of the Jaguar Drivers' Club, wrote that 'many of the brilliant Jaguar advertisements and publicity campaigns were the result of Bill Rankin's fertile mind'.

Bob Berry feels that, 'he was undoubtedly the guy who was responsible for the creation of the whole Jaguar image'.

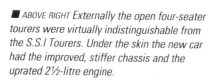

■ *ABOVE RIGHT Externally the open four-seater tourers were virtually indistinguishable from the S.S.I Tourers. Under the skin the new car had the improved, stiffer chassis and the uprated 2½-litre engine.*

retained the 'old' Standard 12 1608-cc side-valve engine. Externally it differed in having shorter front wings and a shorter bonnet. The spare wheel, mounted on both models in the left-hand front wing, protruded above the bonnet line on the smaller version. With its underpowered engine, the car was not exactly sporting, but its level of refinement and 'expensive' style made it popular at a price of just £285.

An open Tourer model with the S.S.I body continued to be produced and now benefited from the new chassis and overhead valve power unit. It is possible that the company was merely using up a stock of bodies; or perhaps it wished to avoid the added complication of introducing an open version of the new saloons at this stage. Whatever the explanation, only about 100 SS Jaguar Tourers were produced during the two years that they were listed, 1936 and 1937.

By far the most exciting car yet produced by the dynamic young company was the SS Jaguar 100, introduced alongside the other new models in late 1935. Similar in shape to the S.S. 90, of which only 24 had been built, the 100 was a far more sporting machine, having the extra power of the overhead valve 2½-litre unit. Like its predecessor, the SS 100 was based on a shortened S.S.I chassis, but the 100 could be distinguished by its slightly raked, rear-mounted slab petrol tank. The tank on the 90 was vertical.

At last there was an SS that was not only a work of timeless beauty but also a splendid performer. Top speed was around 95 mph and 60 mph could be reached from standstill in 13 seconds. The engine produced a little over 100 bhp and possessed excellent flexibility. The price, as ever, defied belief at just £395.

In 1936 the SS began to distinguish itself in the competition world. In the Marne Sports Car Grand Prix at Rheims, McEvoy won his class and the Wisdoms, Bill and Elsie, put up the best individual performance, irrespective of class, in the Alpine Trial. To achieve this they took on and beat much European competition including no fewer than six BMW's. The Coventry distributor, S.H. 'Sammy' Newsome, won the 3000-cc unsupercharged class at Shelsley Walsh in September. In March of the following year Jack Harrop and Bob Taylor won the R.A.C. Rally, beating in the process a works team of SS 100's which took the manufacturer's team prize. In July Jacob put up the best performance in the Welsh Rally and in September the car affectionately known as 'Old No. 8', after its chassis number, which the company had lent to Wisdom for his Alpine success, was fitted with an experimental 3½-litre engine and took Newsome to another success at Shelsley. The same car clocked up another win for Newsome at Brooklands.

As demand for the saloons grew, it became increasingly obvious that

---

♦ S S J A G U A R   1 0 0 ♦

BODY STYLE: Two Seater Sports
ENGINE: Overhead valve 6 cyl,
   2663 & 3485 cc
MAX POWER: 102 bhp & 125 bhp
TIME: 0–60 12.8 secs & 10.9 secs
MAX SPEED: 94 mph & 101 mph
QUANTITY MADE: 198 & 116
PRICE: £395 & £445
ANNOUNCEMENT DATE: Sept 1935
   & Sept 1937
IN PRODUCTION: 1936–1940 & 1938–1940

■ *ABOVE The SS Jaguar 100, generally known today simply as the SS 100, was similar in body design to the S.S. 90 built briefly in 1935. However, like the tourer, the '100' had the new chassis and engine, giving the car virtual 100-mph performance and roadholding to match.*

BILL HEYNES RECALLS

'*I* joined Mr. Lyons, as he then was, on April 5th 1935. As with everything he did, he was very careful in selecting who he had to join his team. I think I had at least six interviews with him and he had interviews with quite a number of other people in the industry before he chose me.

'I think the real reason he chose me was because I called him "sir". Everyone else called him "Bill"! Anyway, I was taken on at the magnificent sum of £600 a year.

Lyons already had the body designed for the first Jaguar. I went to see it with him and was very impressed. He said to me, "We want the works of this car to be as good as the bodywork". That was my job.

'We worked on it day and night, including Sundays. I had tremendous help from Grinham and Dawtrey, my old chiefs at Humber, who were now with Standards. Weslake had done a cylinder head for the Standard engine and I had to do a new bottom end, a new crankshaft and a new oil system. We also designed a new front suspension and a better type of chassis frame plus new brakes. We managed to get it all done, at a scrape, in just five months ready for the launch at the Mayfair Hotel.'

different manufacturing methods were needed if production were to match demand. The traditional coachbuilders' art of using a wooden frame, though Swallow had done more than most to streamline and rationalize the method in the search for efficiency and low costs, was indisputably slow and unsuited to higher volumes of production.

All-steel construction, using an assembly of pressings, was the answer. It was not practical for the still relatively small company to produce the pressings themselves. The Pressed Steel company could have produced the whole body, but it required a lead time of a whole year. This did not suit the fast-moving Lyons, who decided to engage a number of firms to produce components for assembly at SS Cars.

That decision was a disaster which nearly ruined the company. The suppliers were late in fulfilling their orders and many components did not match up as intended. For months the increased workforce was virtually idle while problems were resolved. Eventually they were resolved, compensation was gained from some suppliers and the increased rate of production allowed the company to turn a certain loss into profit. The following year, 1938, brought record profits.

The all-steel saloons, as they are known, remained visually similar to their predecessors. The most noticeable change was the removal of the spare wheel from its front wing mounting to a home initially in the bootlid, later under the boot floor. A new, more rigid, yet slightly lighter chassis was designed by Heynes. Larger doors eased access and the new method of construction gave greater interior space.

As for engines, the 2½ litre had benefited from an increased compression ratio and improved exhaust manifolding, raising power output to the 100 bhp mark. The 1½, however, was a different unit, being based on Standard's 1776-cc four-cylinder as used in the Standard 14. The transition to overhead valves increased output from a modest 45 hp to a more useful 65 hp, giving the SS Jaguar a performance rating 50 per cent higher than its competitors'. Of greater interest was the addition to the range of a 3½-litre engine. It followed the familiar pattern: Weslake's head, two SU carburettors and two triple-branch exhaust manifolds. The extra performance took this model into the true high-performance sporting cars league.

■ *RIGHT Although the SS 100's were not produced in large numbers, they enhanced the image of SS Cars, as the company was now known, immeasurably.*

After the war Ian Appleyard, a Jaguar distributor in the northern town of Leeds who represented his country at skiing in the 1948 Olympic Games, took up rallying.

At first he used his own 1938 3½-litre SS 100 on the Alpine Rally, but the car wore its tyres out at such a rate that he literally ran out of spares.

He then acquired a 'new' 3½-litre SS 100, which had been stored throughout the war at Lyons' home, Wappenbury Hall. This car, registered LNW 100, became particularly well known and recorded the model's greatest successes when the SS 100 was no longer in production. Appleyard entered the new car in the 1948 event. It was in standard form apart from improvements to the steering.

LNW 100

The competition included Allards, Citroens, Delahayes, Hotchkiss, H.R.G.'s and the new Sunbeam-Talbot 90's.

Heavy rain meant slippery conditions and among the casualties was Donald Healey, in a car of his own make, who was saved from a 2000-foot drop by a well-positioned tree! Appleyard saved time en route by having his navigator refuel from cans while on the move, difficult enough on flat, straight roads, but more so on the tortuous Alpine passes! Snow was encountered on the Susten Pass and a herd of cows on another section. But still Appleyard remained on time and

penalty-free. After rushing through a pathway cut through 30-foot snow drifts on the Iseran, the SS Jaguar collected a hen, which perched in front of the radiator for several kilometres before being dislodged on a particularly sharp bend!

Thirty-five minutes were lost when Appleyard's navigator, a doctor, had to minister to an injured competitor. A 64-mph average thus had to be maintained between the mountain town of Grasse and the coastal resort of Cannes.

Appleyard and Potter, in an Allard, were equal at the finish and matters were decided by a short test consisting of accelerating, braking and reversing. The Jaguar driver beat his compatriot by 0.3 seconds and so collected a coveted Coupe des Alpes for a penalty-free run.

■ *LEFT AND ABOVE The SS's found their way into a wide variety of competitions – rallies, hillclimbs, trials and races. One car, considerably modified by the factory as time passed and entered with success at the famous Weybridge track and Shelsley Walsh hillclimb in Worcestershire, became affectionately known, from its chassis number, as 'Old No. 8'. One of its early events was the Alpine Trial in which Tom and Elsie Wisdom (seen here) achieved best overall performance.*

Along with all these changes, Drophead Coupe versions of the 1½, 2½ and 3½ SS Jaguars were added to the line-up. The Dropheads were beautifully made and most stylish. They had two doors and the hood could be opened as far as the rear door pillar into the 'coupe de ville' position or fully folded in the usual way. Not surprisingly, the new 3½ litre was fitted into the SS 100, giving this model a performance that allowed it to compete with even more distinction in international sporting events. In 1938 such cars again won the R.A.C. and Welsh rallies.

Flamboyant in style but imbued with exciting performance, the SS 100 was one of the classic British pre-war sports cars. It was one of the last of the era before streamlining began to influence shape. Indeed, former owners say that the wind used to get 'caught' under those generous SS 100 front wings at speed, making the steering go light!

For the 1938 Earl's Court Show, Lyons did design and show a one-off streamlined SS 100. This closed car, rather reminiscent of certain Bugattis of the period, may have been intended for production. But peace and the progress of SS cars were about to be rudely interrupted. The Coupe was destined to serve only as a pointer towards things to come once hostilities had ceased.

In the latter part of 1939, production of cars was phased out as the SS plant was turned over to war work. But the old faithful sidecars, for which

♦ SS JAGUAR ♦
1½ LITRE SALOON & DROPHEAD COUPE

BODY STYLE(s): All Steel Construction, Four Door Saloon & Two Door Convertible
ENGINE: Overhead valve 4 cyl 1776 cc
MAX POWER: 65 bhp
TIME: 0–60 25.1 secs
MAX SPEED: 71.7 mph
QUANTITY MADE: Saloon 4402 Drophead 675
PRICE: Saloon £298   Drophead £318
ANNOUNCEMENT DATE: Sept 1937
IN PRODUCTION: 1938–1940

■ *ABOVE A new range of SS 100's was introduced late in 1937, though visually they remained similar. The important difference was that these saloons were now of an all-steel construction, which replaced the old method of mounting panels to an ash frame. This method both improved the cars and shortened the hours of production.*

■ *RIGHT The tourers were replaced by Drophead versions of the saloons which were offered, like the saloons, in 1½, 2½- and 3½-litre versions. In spite of their remarkably low prices, these models oozed opulence.*

16 The Motor   July 11, 1939.

GO past traffic like the wind with Jaguar's abounding power and eager response to the throttle. (The 3½ litre has a 95 m.p.h. maximum and reaches 50 m.p.h. from rest in 9½ secs.).

STOP on the dot when your foot says so, with Jaguar's magnificent Girling brakes. Stop swiftly and surely—at the lightest touch on the pedal. (30 feet from 30 m.p.h.).

LOOK where you're going in comfort when you reverse in a Jaguar Drophead Coupe. 'Its head folds down perfectly flat—or goes up again in a matter of seconds.

SEE every inch of the road from the deep and luxurious driving seat. See *both* wings through the broad, deep screen, and adjust that big steering wheel just where you want it.

FEEL the magnificent way your Jaguar sits down on the road. Feel how it corners, with no lurch or sway—how it glides over potholes with scarcely a tremor.

RELAX in that wide, luxurious rear seat—stretch out your legs as you please—finish your journey unfatigued and rejoice in the smooth, silent comfort of your Jaguar!

Everything you demand—more than you expect

At Devonshire House, Piccadilly, Henlys have extensive new showrooms devoted solely to Jaguar cars. Henlys are Jaguar distributors for Southern England and in Manchester. Throughout these areas are many Jaguar agents with excellent delivery and service facilities. 'May we arrange a demonstration?
3½ Litre Saloon £445 (Drophead Coupe £465). 2½ Litre Saloon £395 (Drophead, £415).
1½ Litre Saloon £298 (Drophead, £318).
HENLYS LTD., DEVONSHIRE HOUSE, PICCADILLY, W.1 (GROSVENOR 2955) AND AT MANCHESTER AND BOURNEMOUTH

JAGUAR at HENLYS
A16

♦ SS JAGUAR ♦
2½ LITRE SALOON & DROPHEAD COUPE

BODY STYLE(s): All Steel Construction, Four Door Saloon & Two Door Convertible
ENGINE: Overhead valve 6 cyl, 2663 cc
MAX POWER: 105 bhp
TIME: 0–60 17 secs
MAX SPEED: 87 mph
QUANTITY MADE: Saloon 1577 Drophead 281
PRICE: Saloon £395   Drophead £415
ANNOUNCEMENT DATE: Sept 1938
IN PRODUCTION: 1938–1940

Lyons had formed a separate company entitled Swallow Coachbuilding (1935) Ltd upon going public, had continued to prosper and were to assume renewed importance as production was increased to supply the Army, the Navy, the Air Force and Fire Brigades. Apart from the sidecars, 700 trailers of various sorts were made per week.

Some experimental work was carried out, but the major concentration of effort centred on aircraft work, for which significant new techniques were learned and more sophisticated machine tools acquired. The famous Whitley and Wellington bombers were repaired and parts such as wings, cockpit roofs, bomb doors, tanks, formers and frames were manufactured for the legendary Spitfires, Lancasters, Stirlings and Mosquitos. Thousands of parts were made for aircraft guns and towards the end of the war, 98 complete centre sections were produced for the revolutionary Gloster Meteor III jet fighter.

Just before war broke out, Wally Hassan, a former Bentley apprentice and the designer of distinguished Brooklands specials, had joined the company. Finding little to stretch him in the early period of the war, he left

■ *ABOVE Although it was stated after the war that production of the SS 100 would recommence, none was, in fact, produced and no sports car was made until 1948.*

♦ S S J A G U A R ♦
3½ LITRE SALOON &
DROPHEAD COUPE

BODY STYLE(s): All Steel Construction,
  Four Door Saloon &
  Two Door Convertible
ENGINE: Overhead valve 6 cyl, 3485 cc
MAX POWER: 125 bhp
TIME: 0–60 9 secs
MAX SPEED: 91.8 mph
QUANTITY MADE: Saloon 1065
  Drophead 239
PRICE: Saloon £445   Drophead £465
ANNOUNCEMENT DATE: Sept 1937
IN PRODUCTION: 1938–1940

■ *LEFT One SS 100 had been stored at Lyons' home, Wappenbury Hall, during the war and in the late 1940s it was acquired by Ian Appleyard, who rallied the car – LNW 100 – with great success, most notably when he won the 1948 Alpine Rally.*

■ *ABOVE As the company went from strength to strength, the workforce increased in numbers and some production methods changed. Ash frames were no longer employed (except for Drophead models) and all-steel body construction was adopted. Many of the operations, such as trimming, nevertheless remained, as they do today, highly skilled jobs. A few years after the war the company, its name now simply Jaguar, moved on from the Foleshill factory seen here.*

■ *LEFT The SS Jaguar 100's pure, clean lines give the car a simple beauty that few others of any age have matched. It was Lyons' pre-war masterpiece.*

in search of new challenges but returned in 1943 to work on small, light vehicles which could be dropped by parachute. Two were built. The first, entitled the VA, had a rear-mounted V-twin JAP motorcycle engine and the second, the VB, a more powerful Ford unit. The significance of these vehicles is that apart from having independent suspension all round, they had no chassis. But the body, such as it was, was stressed like that of a modern car.

In an endeavour to become self-sufficient in body-panel supply, Lyons had purchased, just before the war, one of his major suppliers, Motor Panels Ltd. The company was not a great success, however, and, needing funds to resurrect vehicle production as peace returned, he sold the company to Rubery Owen. If he had not done so the story of the British motor industry might have been very different. Lyons made another shrewd move in the last days of the war. When Sir John Black of Standard stated that he would no longer be able to supply the 2½- and 3½-litre engines as before, Lyons offered to buy the machine tools. He moved fast to conclude the deal and gave Black no time for reflection. Black was later to regret his decision, but

◆ J A G U A R ◆
1½ LITRE SALOON &
DROPHEAD COUPE

BODY STYLE: As Pre-War cars
ENGINE: Overhead valve 4 cyl, 1776 cc
MAX POWER: 65 bhp
TIME: 0–60 25.1 secs
MAX SPEED: 71.7 mph
QUANTITY MADE: Saloon 5761
      Drophead - Not Available
PRICE: Saloon £684
      Drophead - Not Available
ANNOUNCEMENT DATE: July 1945
IN PRODUCTION: 1945–1949

■ *ABOVE, LEFT AND RIGHT The pre-war models were reintroduced after the war in virtually unchanged form. All three engine sizes and Drophead models of each were still produced.*

♦JAGUAR♦
2½ LITRE SALOON &
DROPHEAD COUPE

BODY STYLE(s): As Pre-War cars
ENGINE: Overhead valve 6 cyl, 2663 cc
MAX POWER: 105 bhp
TIME: 0–60 17 secs
MAX SPEED: 87 mph
QUANTITY MADE: Saloon 1757
    Drophead 104
PRICE: Saloon £889   Drophead £1189
ANNOUNCEMENT DATE: Saloon July 1945
    Drophead Dec 1947
IN PRODUCTION: Saloon 1946–1949
    Drophead 1948

♦JAGUAR♦
3½ LITRE SALOON &
DROPHEAD COUPE

BODY STYLE(s): As Pre-War cars
ENGINE: Overhead valve 6 cyl, 3485 cc
MAX POWER: 125 bhp
TIME: 0–60 16.8 secs
MAX SPEED: 91 mph
QUANTITY MADE: Saloon 3860
    Drophead 560
PRICE: Saloon £991   Drophead £1263
ANNOUNCEMENT DATE: Saloon July 1945
    Drophead Dec 1947
IN PRODUCTION: Saloon 1946–1949
    Drophead 1947–1948

Lyons was now self-sufficient, apart from having to buy in the 1½-litre engine.

Early in 1945 the company name was changed to Jaguar Cars Ltd. The initials 'SS' now had unpleasant connotations and were dropped for good. The Swallow sidecar division was sold off and all effort was concentrated on getting cars into production again – not an easy business in a time of shortages and steel quotas. The steel quotas were designed to encourage firms to export and Lyons and his colleagues took up that challenge as successfully as any other company, if not more so.

William Heynes was appointed to the board at this time and Claude Baily, who had joined the company at the beginning of the war, became his Chief Engineer. Another famous Jaguar name entered the scene in 1946, when an unusually tall young man known as Lofty England joined the firm. From a racing background which included competing and preparing cars for Earl Howe, Dick Seaman and E.R.A., England became Jaguar's Service Manager.

In mid-1945 the pre-war saloons once more became available to a British market labouring under petrol rationing. The models were little changed and not easy to distinguish from their pre-war counterparts, though the SS on the wheel spinners was replaced by the Jaguar name and the waist-moulding was rather thinner. The 3½ proved popular in the United States and helped the marque to become established there. The introduction of left-hand drive models and, from late 1947, the Drophead models no doubt helped the export drive. In fact about 35 per cent of total production left Great Britain's shores between 1946 and 1949.

For 1949 Jaguar announced its first 'new' post-war saloon design, though this was to be cautiously evolutionary rather than revolutionary. This, Lyons felt, was the sensible course in what were still difficult times. Even so, his new sports car was distinctly adventurous. A new, extremely stiff, box-section chassis was employed and for the first time independent front suspension appeared on a production Jaguar. It used long torsion bars as the springing

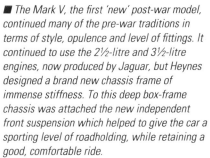

■ The Mark V, the first 'new' post-war model, continued many of the pre-war traditions in terms of style, opulence and level of fittings. It continued to use the 2½-litre and 3½-litre engines, now produced by Jaguar, but Heynes designed a brand new chassis frame of immense stiffness. To this deep box-frame chassis was attached the new independent front suspension which helped to give the car a sporting level of roadholding, while retaining a good, comfortable ride.

♦ **JAGUAR MARK V** ♦
2½ LITRE SALOON &
DROPHEAD COUPE

BODY STYLE(s): Four Door Saloon and
    Two Door Convertible
ENGINE: Overhead valve 6 cyl, 2663 cc
MAX POWER: 102 bhp
TIME: 0–60 17 secs
MAX SPEED: 87 mph
QUANTITY MADE: Saloon 1647
    Drophead 28
PRICE: Saloon £1189 (1949)
    Drophead £1247 (1950)
ANNOUNCEMENT DATE: Oct 1948
IN PRODUCTION: 1949–1950

medium, rather like the Citroen which Heynes had always admired. The smallest engine was no longer available since Standard had ceased production, thus ending an historic association; and so the new Mark V was made available with a choice of 2½- or 3½-litre engines.

A Drophead variant was also offered, but of the thousand or so made in the years 1949-51 only just over 100 remained in Great Britain. The Mark V's, which offered a good performance, respectable roadholding, a high level of appointments and, as ever, remarkable value for money were the last of what might be termed the traditional pre-war cars from the Coventry company.

■ *ABOVE AND RIGHT The Mark V was a sensible compromise in difficult economic times. Immediately after the war Jaguar did not have the resources to develop a completely new and radical saloon.*

♦ C O L O U R   S C H E M E S ♦

The colour schemes listed below are standard, and any deviation involving special treatment of coachwork and/or upholstery will entail extra charges for which a quotation will be given at the time of ordering.

D R O P H E A D   C O U P E   M O D E L S

CODE NO.	COACHWORK	INTERIOR	HOOD
COUPE 1	SUEDE GREEN	SUEDE GREEN	FRENCH GREY
COUPE 2	SUEDE GREEN	SUEDE GREEN	BLACK
COUPE 3	IVORY	RED	DARK SAND
COUPE 4	IVORY	RED	BLACK
COUPE 5	IVORY	PALE BLUE	FRENCH GREY
COUPE 6	IVORY	PALE BLUE	BLACK
COUPE 7	BIRCH GREY	RED	FRENCH GREY
COUPE 8	BIRCH GREY	RED	BLACK
COUPE 9	BIRCH GREY	GREY	FRENCH GREY
COUPE 10	BIRCH GREY	GREY	BLACK
COUPE 11	BIRCH GREY	PALE BLUE	FRENCH GREY
COUPE 12	BIRCH GREY	PALE BLUE	BLACK
COUPE 13	BATTLESHIP GREY	RED	FRENCH GREY
COUPE 14	BATTLESHIP GREY	RED	GUNMETAL
COUPE 15	BATTLESHIP GREY	RED	BLACK
COUPE 16	BATTLESHIP GREY	GREY	FRENCH GREY
COUPE 17	BATTLESHIP GREY	GREY	GUNMETAL
COUPE 18	BATTLESHIP GREY	GREY	BLACK
COUPE 19	LAVENDER GREY	RED	FRENCH GREY
COUPE 20	LAVENDER GREY	RED	BLACK
COUPE 21	LAVENDER GREY	SUEDE GREEN	FRENCH GREY
COUPE 22	LAVENDER GREY	SUEDE GREEN	BLACK
COUPE 23	LAVENDER GREY	PALE BLUE	FRENCH GREY
COUPE 24	LAVENDER GREY	PALE BLUE	BLACK
COUPE 25	GUNMETAL	RED	FRENCH GREY
COUPE 26	GUNMETAL	RED	GUNMETAL
COUPE 27	GUNMETAL	RED	BLACK
COUPE 28	GUNMETAL	GREY	FRENCH GREY
COUPE 29	GUNMETAL	GREY	GUNMETAL
COUPE 30	GUNMETAL	GREY	BLACK
COUPE 31	GUNMETAL	PALE BLUE	FRENCH GREY
COUPE 32	GUNMETAL	PALE BLUE	GUNMETAL
COUPE 33	GUNMETAL	PALE BLUE	BLACK
COUPE 34	BLACK	TAN	DARK SAND
COUPE 35	BLACK	TAN	FRENCH GREY
COUPE 36	BLACK	TAN	BLACK
COUPE 37	BLACK	RED	FRENCH GREY
COUPE 38	BLACK	RED	BLACK
COUPE 39	BLACK	RED	DARK SAND
COUPE 40	BLACK	GREY	FRENCH GREY
COUPE 41	BLACK	GREY	BLACK
COUPE 42	BLACK	GREY	GUNMETAL
COUPE 43	BLACK	PIGSKIN GRAIN	DARK SAND
COUPE 44	BLACK	PIGSKIN GRAIN	FRENCH GREY
COUPE 45	BLACK	PIGSKIN GRAIN	BLACK
COUPE 46	BLACK	BISCUIT	DARK SAND
COUPE 47	BLACK	BISCUIT	FRENCH GREY
COUPE 48	BLACK	BISCUIT	BLACK
COUPE 49	PASTEL GREEN METALLIC	SUEDE GREEN	FRENCH GREY
COUPE 50	PASTEL GREEN METALLIC	GREY	FRENCH GREY
COUPE 51	PASTEL GREEN METALLIC	GREY	BLACK
COUPE 52	PASTEL BLUE METALLIC	PALE BLUE	FRENCH GREY
COUPE 53	PASTEL BLUE METALLIC	PALE BLUE	BLACK
COUPE 54	PASTEL BLUE METALLIC	GREY	FRENCH GREY
COUPE 55	PASTEL BLUE METALLIC	GREY	BLACK
COUPE 56	DOVE GREY	TAN	DARK SAND
COUPE 57	DOVE GREY	TAN	BLACK
COUPE 58	DOVE GREY	BISCUIT	DARK SAND
COUPE 59	DOVE GREY	BISCUIT	BLACK

♦ J A G U A R   M A R K   V ♦
3½ L I T R E   S A L O O N   &
D R O P H E A D   C O U P E

BODY STYLE(s): Four door saloon and Two Door Convertible
ENGINE: Overhead valve 6 cyl, 3485 cc
MAX POWER: 125 bhp
TIME: 0–60 14.7 secs
MAX SPEED: 92 mph
QUANTITY MADE: Saloon 7814
    Drophead 977
PRICE: Saloon £1263
ANNOUNCEMENT DATE: Oct 1948
IN PRODUCTION: 1949–1951

■ *LEFT Jaguar offered a bewildering array of 59 standard colour schemes to tempt buyers.*

■ *RIGHT The British Government exhorted manufacturers to give top priority to exports. The Mark V Dropheads led the way for Jaguar and achieved useful sales in the United States, which was about to become Jaguar's most important market.*

CHAPTER THREE

THE EXCITING XK'S

The celebrated XK120 was the first of the line and in 1948 the fastest production car in the world.

*A*s Lyons' aspirations grew, the next logical step was for his company to design and produce its own high-performance engine. It now controlled the manufacture of the former Standard engines, but in spite of Weslake's and Heynes' improvements these were now elderly engines, far from advanced in concept. The thrusting Jaguar concern needed a new power unit to trounce its rivals, one which was advanced in conception. Such a unit would finally lay to rest any jibe about the Jaguar having more promise of performance than reality.

Throughout the war, small teams of employees were organized on a shift basis to carry out factory fire-watching in case of aerial attack. Lyons took his turn and used these boring sessions to plan for the future. He organized the shifts so that Heynes, Hassan and Baily should share duties with him from 6 pm on Sunday evenings. Lyons would talk of his vision for the coming years: from the outset a power output of 160 bhp, excellent torque, smooth refinement, an advanced specification and a stylish external appearance were the criteria that Lyons laid down for his engineers.

With concern about post-war petrol rationing and the fear that taxation might discriminate against larger engines, the size initially chosen was 2½ litres. This unit was to have six cylinders and there was to be a smaller one with four cylinders. Each model was to have certain shared dimensions, thereby enabling the same machinery to produce either.

The designs were given initials to distinguish them, starting with XA, the X standing for experimental. The first to get further than the drawing board was the sixth version, the XF. This four-cylinder engine had a capacity of 1360 cc but, significantly, had hemispherical combustion chambers and twin overhead camshafts. Overhead cams had, on the whole, been the preserve of racing engines and a few of the more exotic Italian makes. Such a configuration was considered far too sophisticated for 'production' cars, especially those that would need to be worked on in all corners of the world if Lyons' plans succeeded. Lyons, however, liked the idea – it fitted his concept of the new Jaguar image – and he encouraged his engineers to work along these lines.

SPECIAL EQUIPMENT XK 120 MODELS

*T*he specification is similar to that for standard XK120 models, with the following departures: Special camshafts with ⅜in lift. Special crankshaft damper. Wire spoke wheels with splined hubs and knock-on hub caps. Dual exhaust system (on Open Model only).
Stiffer torsion bars of 1in diameter

ALTERNATIVE EQUIPMENT
The following equipment is available at extra cost:
BODY: Racing windscreen and cowl; bucket seats
ENGINE: Modified cylinder head, having larger valves and valve throats and modified porting; available with large (2 in) bore carburettors.
CLUTCH: Special racing clutch.
GEARBOX: Close-ratio gearbox, giving the following ratios (compared with the standard gearbox):

CLOSE RATIO:

First	2.98
Second	1.74
Third	1.21
Top	Direct

STANDARD RATIO

First	3.375
Second	1.982
Third	1.367
Top	Direct

AXLE: Alternative axles are available giving the following ratios: 3.31, (3.54), 4.09, 4.27, 4.55.
TYRES: Dunlop Road Racing Tyres.
FUEL SYSTEM: Additional tankage to bring total capacity up to 24 gallons – supplied with additional fuel pump. (This tank considerably reduces the luggage accommodation.)

This information is reproduced from the 'Salesman's Data Book'. These models became available at the same time as the XK120 FHCs in 1951, producing 190 bhp and known in the States as the XK120M (for Modified). The improved 'C-type' (for Competition) cylinder head was fitted to competition models known as XK120MCs.

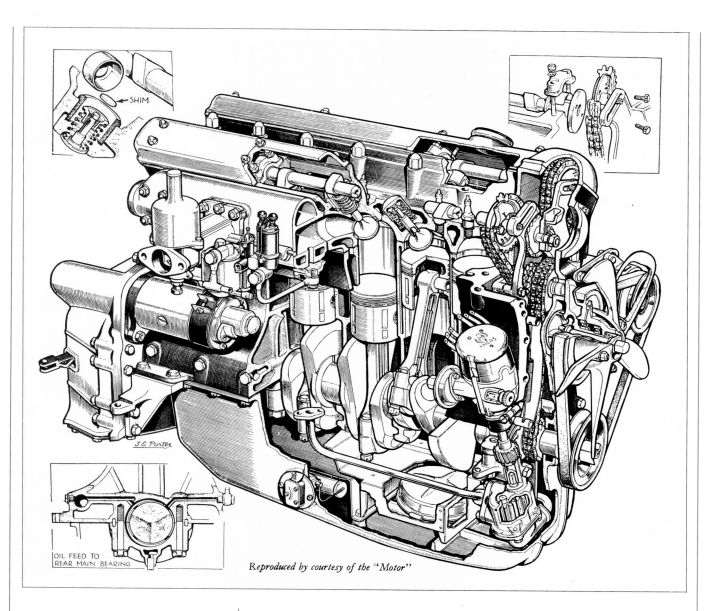

SHIM

OIL FEED TO
REAR MAIN BEARING

S.G.Porter

Reproduced by courtesy of the "Motor"

■ *ABOVE It is hard to describe the significance
of the XK engine and impossible to overstate its
importance to Jaguar. It was the engine that
was to put the company on the world map and
on which virtually all its products were based
for nearly forty years.*

■ *LEFT The XK120 was undoubtedly a
glamorous car but, with its performance, the
beauty was more than skin deep!*

The XF suffered from a lack of block strength and so a further prototype
was built. The XG, which employed a single side camshaft in the block
similar to contemporary BMW methods, was built on the 1776-cc Standard
engine. It proved to be too noisy. Hence the 2-litre XJ with twin overhead
cams was constructed and considerable development work carried out. The
lessons were applied to a 3182-cc six-cylinder version of the XJ and, apart
from a lack of torque, this model seemed most satisfactory. To overcome the
torque problems, the stroke was increased, giving a final capacity of 3442 cc
and this unit, known as the XK, was to be the final specification.

This new engine was designed for a completely new range of saloons
which would not make their debut until 1951. It had been decided that it
would weaken the impact of the new engine to introduce it in the stop-gap
Mark V's. However the Mark V's had an excellent new chassis with the new
independent front suspension and, since the demise of the SS 100 because of
the war, Jaguar had no sports car on offer. Such cars might not make a great
deal of profit, but they gained excellent publicity. Furthermore, the few who

◆ N O T E S   O N   T H E   J A G U A R   X K   T Y P E   E N G I N E ◆
By W. M. HEYNES, M.I.Mech.E., M.S.A.E.
Chief Engineer, Jaguar Cars Ltd.

In this new range of Jaguar engines all compromise in design has been eliminated. Each engine can be truthfully stated to incorporate all the most advanced technical knowledge available today on naturally aspirated petrol engines. Tests carried out on the completed units have shown the wisdom of the decision taken by the Jaguar Company nearly nine years ago to develop an engine on these lines.

In addition to bench tests, totalling many thousands of hours, extensive road tests at home and abroad have been carried out, and it is significant that the 2 litre engine, loaned to Colonel Gardner when he broke the world speed record in the 2 litre class at 176 miles per hour, is a completely standard unit with the exception of modified pistons to give a higher compression ratio. Further proof of the high efficiency of the XK engine was provided on the 30th of May, 1949, when an entirely standard production 3½ Litre Model running on pump petrol obtained a speed of 132.6 mph under the official observation of the Royal Automobile Club of Belgium. This speed is the highest ever recorded by a standard production car.

From the following condensed resumé of the more important features of the Type XK engine, it will be seen that no reliance has been placed upon the use of new or untried inventions. Instead, a blend of known and proved detail designs of the highest efficiency has resulted in the creation of a production engine of unparalleled quality and performance.

The following are some of the more important points:

(1) Hemispherical head of high strength aluminium alloy with large diameter valves set 70°; the sparking plugs are disposed on the engine centre line in the path of the incoming gases. This ensures complete and rapid burning of the mixture, and ensures regular firing at slow speed pulling or maximum rpm.

VALVE SEATINGS:

(2) These are of special high expansion cast-iron in which the coefficient of expansion approximates to that of the alloy cylinder head. This construction ensures a rapid flow of heat from the valve seat, eliminating local over-heating and giving an exceptional life to both valves and seatings.

INDUCTION SYSTEM:

(3) The valve ports and induction system have been designed in collaboration with Mr. Harry Weslake (generally accepted as the foremost expert in this science) and combine large induction passages, which offer a minimum restriction to flow, with specially contoured ports which ensure a controlled degree of turbulence in the combustion chamber.

TWIN OVERHEAD CAMSHAFTS:

(4) Twin overhead camshafts, driven by two-stage chains, act directly on the valves through floating tappets. This reduces to a minimum the unsprung weight of the valve parts and enables extremely light valve springs to operate satisfactorily up to the high maximum rpm. In addition, the absence of rockers and push rods eliminate the main source of wear and noise often associated with overhead valve mechanisms. The camshaft and tappet face are submerged in an oil bath formed in the cylinder head casting, which forms an oil cushion between the two working surfaces.

OILING SYSTEM:

(5) Large capacity oil pump is driven by skew gears on the front of the crankshaft and picks up oil from the sump through a floating strainer, which avoids cavitation, whilst the strainer ensures that no particles of dirt can enter the oiling system. On the delivery side of the pump all the oil is passed through a full-flow pressure filter and from there into a ¾″ diameter gallery, which runs the full length of the engine and from which distribution throughout the engine is taken.

COOLING SYSTEM:

(6) Water circulation is supplied by high pressure centrifugal pump on the input side of the engine. This avoids any chance of steam pocketing, which can occur when the pump is used as an extractor. The water is fed from the pump down a separate gallery on the nearside of the cylinder block, and jets are directed on to the exhaust valve seatings and so across the head, around the sparking plugs, past the inlet valves, and passing out to the radiator through a gallery cast integral with the induction pipe. The block is cooled by a restricted circulation which gives a quick warm-up and maintains an efficient operating temperature under running conditions. The radiator block is of a film interspace type and is fitted with a thermostat control with a by-pass which controls the engine temperature.

CRANKSHAFT:

(7) High tensile alloy steel forging with balance weights forged integral with the webs. The seven main bearings on the six-cylinder engines and the three main bearings on the four-cylinder engines are of 2¾″ diameter. The exceptionally large diameter of these bearings and the resulting crank rigidity are responsible to a large degree for the extreme smoothness with which these engines deliver their power, even up to the high maximum rpm of which they are capable.

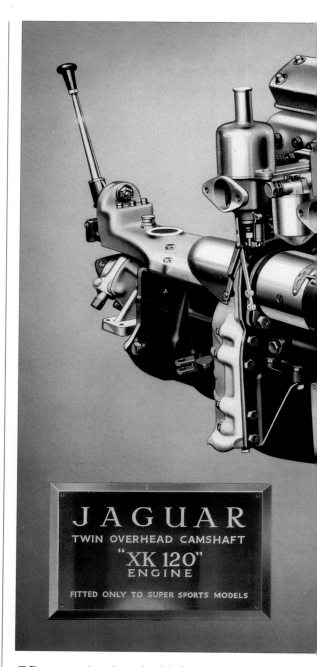

JAGUAR
TWIN OVERHEAD CAMSHAFT
"XK 120"
ENGINE
FITTED ONLY TO SUPER SPORTS MODELS

■ *The move to the twin overhead design was a brave one for 1948, but its successful application over the next 38 years proves just how right the decision was. The technical specification and illustration are taken from the original XK120 brochure.*

SOME WORLD PRESS OPINIONS ON THE XK 120 JAGUAR

The speed achieved (by the Jaguar) is so far ahead of current sports car performance that it represents a major achievement by the British Motor Industry.

Harold Nockolds **THE TIMES**

Jaguar have established their car as the world's fastest unsupercharged catalogue model with full touring bodywork. Indeed, it is very doubtful whether any standard model in catalogue condition, even with the aid of a supercharger, has ever recorded such speeds.

AUTOCAR

The Jaguar Super Sports has thus proved by official timing that it constitutes today the world's fastest unsupercharged production car equipped with a full complete touring body. Moreover, we do not think that any other production car, even supercharged, has ever been officially timed at a higher speed. It can, therefore, be regarded in a manner of speaking, as holding the "Blue Riband" of the road. (Translation)

L'ECHO DE LA BOURSE

The new 3.5 litre Jaguar constitutes one of the most powerful cars produced in England. (Translation)

Berne, **REVUEW-AUTOMOBIEL**

Powered by a 3½-litre twin ohc 160 bhp engine, the Jaguar type XK 120 is an obvious contestant for the title of the world's fastest sports car.

MOTOR

It is typically British that Jaguars never claimed more than 120 mph for this car.

CALIFORNIAN AUTONEWS

One of the most admirable cars is certainly the new Sports Jaguar. Apart from its technical features . . . this car reaches a standard of functional beauty never before achieved by a British manufacturer. As a prestige earner abroad it is probably the most important new car to be shown by the British Industry.

J. Eason Gibson, **COUNTRY LIFE**

BEARINGS:

(8) The bearings are the Vandervell thin steel shell white metal lined type for crankshaft, connecting rods and camshaft bearings, and although these are precision made and completely interchangeable without fitting, they have proved to give practically unlimited life under more exacting test conditions.

PISTONS:

(9) High strength aluminium alloy fitted with two narrow compression rings, the top ring being chromium plated to eliminate corrosion and consequent wear and, in addition, a slotted oil control ring is also fitted.

CONNECTING RODS:

(10) Steel "H" section forging drilled up the centre web to provide oil feed to small end. The big end and cap are well ribbed to give rigidity and maintain true circular form under working stresses.

bought a limited run of sports cars would be enthusiasts who, being a tolerant lot, would be ideal guinea pigs for the new engine. Hence the XK120 was born. The Mark V chassis was shortened and Lyons rapidly designed a body in time for the 1948 Motor Show. The XK120 was the star of the show and was destined to become one of the few all-time classics.

The car promised excitement in a period of austerity. It was even talked about as a morale booster and prestige earner for British industry. Such were the claims for the performance and top speed, on which the name was based, that few believed them; press and public alike thought them wildly exaggerated. This was racing car performance. In spite of the lack of credibility, the orders poured in and it was realized even during the show that the original intended batch of around 200 aluminium-bodied cars would in no way satisfy demand. The decision was therefore taken to 'tool up' for pressed-steel bodies and this, plus further development, inevitably took time. Very few XK's saw the light of day until the early fifties, and then

the greater proportion went across the sea to earn badly-needed dollars.

The intention had been to offer the smaller engine in a version entitled the XK100, but for various reasons only one was ever made. It has been suggested that the machinery did not readily lend itself to manufacturing both engines, that Lyons decided against the car at the last moment or, simply, that demand for the '120' was such that there was no need for, nor the time to produce, the '100'. The XK120 set new standards in performance, styling, roadholding and value for money. What was equally astonishing was that this was no stark, harsh, uncomfortable and impractical racer requiring great strength and ability to pilot. On the contrary, it drew lavish praise for its comfortable ride and docility. The XK120 Super Sports, as the car was originally called, is today known simply as the XK120 Roadster. It was very much a two-seater – with a removable hood, sidescreens and windscreen.

Two events that took place in 1949 silenced those who doubted the car's

♦ **J A G U A R   X K 1 2 0** ♦
O P E N   T W O   S E A T E R
S U P E R   S P O R T S

BODY STYLE(s): Open Roadster with
Rudimentary Hood
ENGINE: XK Twin overhead cam
6 cyl, 3442 cc
MAX POWER: 160 bhp
TIME: 0–60 10 secs
MAX SPEED: 120 mph
QUANTITY MADE: 1175 (rhd) 6437 (lhd)
PRICE: £1263
ANNOUNCEMENT DATE: Oct 1948
IN PRODUCTION: 1949–1954

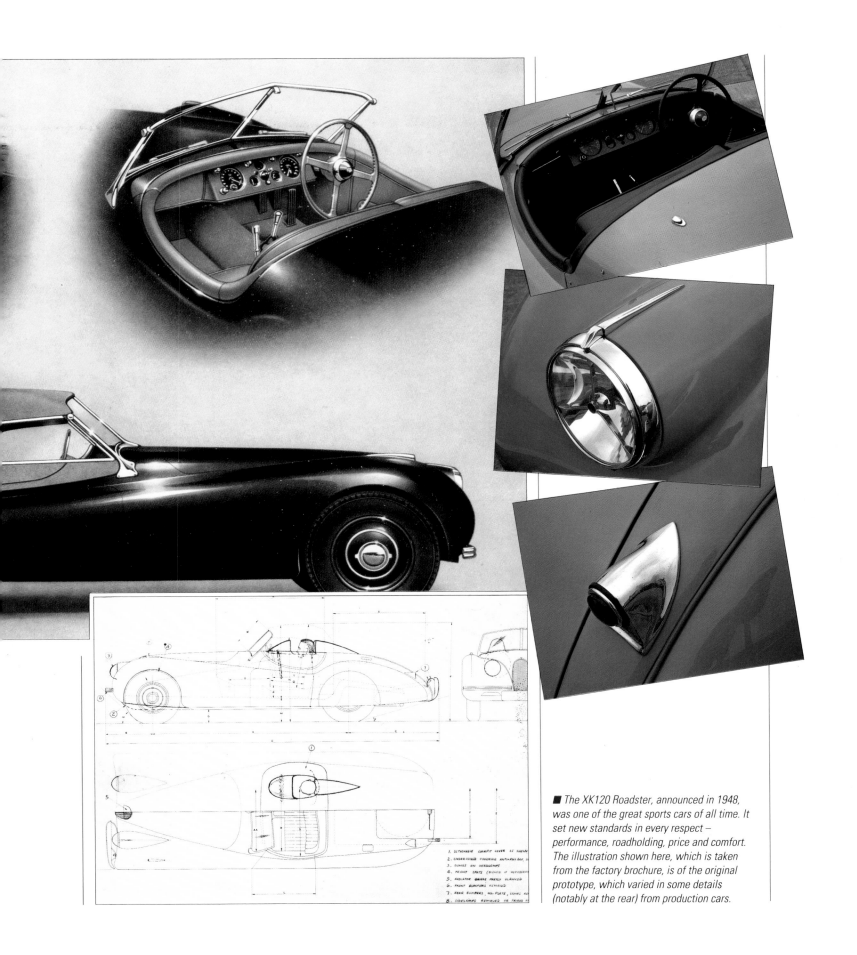

■ The XK120 Roadster, announced in 1948, was one of the great sports cars of all time. It set new standards in every respect – performance, roadholding, price and comfort. The illustration shown here, which is taken from the factory brochure, is of the original prototype, which varied in some details (notably at the rear) from production cars.

performance. First, in May Lyons assembled a party of journalists and flew them out to Jabbeke in Belgium, where 'Soapy' Sutton, the works test driver, proceeded to achieve an officially timed 126 mph with full weather equipment. With a small cowl replacing the windscreen and a metal cover over the passenger compartment, he recorded almost 133 mph. And he completed the display by pottering past the party at 10 mph in fourth gear! In August a race was organized for production sports cars at Silverstone. After a demonstration by Hassan and England some time before the event, Lyons was convinced that the XK's would not disgrace themselves and he lent three models to leading drivers. Leslie Johnson won from Peter Walker and only a puncture stopped Prince Bira from making it a 1-2-3 for the Jaguars. The Publicity Department was not slow to capitalize on that achievement. The task was not difficult, and the press of many nations competed with one another to extol the virtues of this magnificent British car.

As production began to catch up with demand, Jaguar introduced a closed version of the XK120 in 1951. The Fixed Head Coupe not only had a metal roof but was also more luxuriously appointed. Indeed, the interior was more akin to that of the saloons, which had retained that pre-war air of opulence and fine craftsmanship that has been a hallmark of Jaguars to the present day. The XK120 Fixed Head had a figured walnut dashboard and similar door cappings – to say nothing of its wind-up windows.

The roof blended most successfully with the roadster shape and made the car reminiscent of the one-off pre-war SS100 Coupe and Type 57 Bugatti.

■ *ABOVE The Americans took to the XK120 immediately. Many Hollywood stars owned models, enhancing Jaguar's image and sales. In the early days most XK120's went across the Atlantic; very few stayed in Britain. Many of those that did remain were used competitively, as they were in the United States, where drivers like Phil Hill, later to be world champion, cut their teeth on them. Lyons appreciated the publicity that competition success brought to the company. For publicity purposes, Jaguar even exhibited a gold-plated XK.*

■ *ABOVE Jaguar had important markets in Australia and many European countries, where the 'Jag-wah' was becoming even better known.*

■ *BELOW Many people believed that the XK120 brought racing car performance to the road, a view borne out by this model, which achieved 132.6 mph in 1949.*

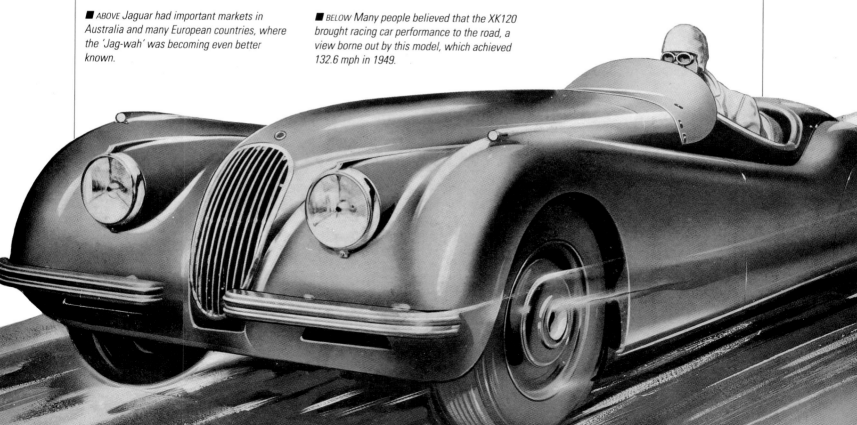

7 DAYS AND 7 NIGHTS

*I*n search of further publicity, Bill Heynes sent his personal XK120 Fixed Head Coupe, chassis number two, registration number LWK 707, to Montlhery. A Shell Oil brochure described the event, before going on to give an engineer's report on the engine. 'On the afternoon of Tuesday, August 5th, 1952, a production model Jaguar XK120 began circling the Montlhery track in France. Seven days and nights later it had made motoring history. The Jaguar had been driven non-stop for 168 hours at over 100 m.p.h.

The night-and-day drivers who put up this magnificent performance for Britain were Leslie Johnson (leader of the team), Stirling Moss, J.E.G. Fairman, H. L. Hadley. By concentrating two years' motoring (16,800 miles) into one week and doing it all at over 100 m.p.h. these British drivers demonstrated the supreme quality of Jaguar engineering.'

The company's racing mechanic, Frank Rainbow, was shown the stripped engine and reported little if any sign of wear to the crankshaft or cylinder bores. All pistons were in good condition and all valves were seating perfectly. The pump was free from sludge and the cylinder head was virtually free from deposits. Not surprisingly, this exercise netted considerable publicity and four world and five class records. It was indeed a genuine testimonial to Jaguar engineering and Shell Oil.

It served to broaden the XK market, though for the first couple of years the models were all exported; for it was not until 1953 that the first right-hand drive model was sold. Fewer than 200 were made in this form and the right-hand drive F.H.C. is a rare model today. With its sophisticated heating and ventilation, plus protection from the elements, the XK120 Fixed Head made a splendid grand touring car, ideal for long continental journeys.

Lyons understood the publicity value of competition success and he was determined that failure should not undermine his hard-earned image. Consequently he often followed a policy of 'lending' factory-prepared cars to carefully selected competitors. In this way he could hardly lose. If they were successful, it was a Jaguar car that had done well. If they did not distinguish themselves, it was merely a private effort which had come to nought.

Thus, in 1950, six special aluminium XK's were supplied to six drivers. The drivers, Leslie Johnson, Tommy Wisdom, Nick Haines, Clement Biondetti, Peter Walker and Ian Appleyard, campaigned 'their' cars far and wide in all manner of events.

Johnson finished fifth in the 1950 Mille Miglia and took his car to Le Mans. He was extremely unlucky not to win this most famous event with his

♦ JAGUAR XK120 ♦
FIXED HEAD COUPE

BODY STYLE(s): Closed Two Seater Coupe
ENGINE: XK Twin overhead cam
 6 cyl, 3442 cc
MAX POWER: 160 bhp
TIME: 0–60 9.9 secs
MAX SPEED: 120 mph
QUANTITY MADE: 195 (rhd) 2484 (lhd)
PRICE: £1775
ANNOUNCEMENT DATE: March 1951
IN PRODUCTION: 1951–1954

■ *The XK120 Roadster body lent itself very well to the Fixed Coupe treatment, which produced a stylish, fast, yet rather more sophisticated, XK, ideal for long-distance touring or competitions.*

relatively standard 120. He retired after 21 hours while catching the leader at a rate which would have taken the XK into the lead before the full 24 hours had elapsed. Two other XK's finished in 12th and 15th places.

Appleyard won the over 3000-cc class and a Coupe des Alpes for a penalty-free run in the tough Alpine Rally of 1950, and Wisdom lent his 120 to a young man called Stirling Moss for the classic T.T. Moss repaid his faith by winning the Tourist Trophy in the most appalling conditions, doing his reputation no end of good in the process.

In August Peter Walker won a one-hour race at Silverstone and a month later he won his class at the legendary Shelsley Walsh hillclimb. Two months later, the future World Champion, Phil Hill, recorded the XK's debut win in the United States with first place in the Pebble Beach Cup Race, California.

■ *The XK120's versatility and its success in competitions and record-breaking is well illustrated by this montage taken from the factory brochure.*

107 m.p.h. for 24 hours at Montlhery, France, 1950. Driven by Leslie Johnson and Stirling Moss.

Leslie Johnson's Jaguar making fastest lap of race at Silverstone, 1949.

Peter Walker's Jaguar winning Production Car Race, Unlimited Class, Silverstone, 1950.

Stirling Moss winning the R.A.C. Tourist Trophy in N. Ireland, 1950.

Leslie Johnson wins 1-hour Production Car Race, Silverstone, 1949.

Ian Appleyard's Jaguar winning Alpine Cup and making best performance Alpine Trial, 1950.

Fastest Production Car in the world.   Start of the 132.6 m.p.h. record, Belgium, 1949.

■ The Silverstone Grand Prix circuit in Great Britain was to become a happy hunting ground for Jaguars, starting with a victory for the XK120s in their first race, in 1949. The photograph of the Leslie Johnson winning car (TOP LEFT) shows the polished camshaft covers which contributed so much to the glamorous appearance of the engine. Later engines had additional studs at the front of the cam covers. White steering wheels (LEFT) were fitted mainly to export models. Peter Walker (ABOVE) continued the winning tradition at Silverstone a year later.

In 1951 XK's occupied the first three positions in the French Rallye Soleil. Appleyard won the Tulip, Morecambe and R.A.C. Rallies, Moss headed home a 1-2-3 at Silverstone, and Appleyard repeated his Alpine success. XK's also won such diverse events as the Liege-Rome-Liege Rally, the Tour de France and the Watkins Glen G.P.

Norman Dewis, Jaguar's chief tester, took a somewhat modified 120 to Jabbeke and proceeded to record an officially observed and timed 172 mph! Competition successes continued to be clocked up all over the world for many years to come.

In April 1953 the XK120 range was expanded with another variation on the theme. The Drophead Coupe was a more sophisticated open version than the Roadster, having a lined folding hood and the opulent interior of the Fixed Head. It was less an out-and-out sports car, and rather more

■ *The Roadster model was somewhat stark by Jaguar standards (though not by normal sports car standards), with rather rudimentary sidescreens and removable hood. A more sophisticated open XK joined the range in 1953, when the Drophead Coupe model, with folding hood and wind-up windows, was introduced.*

■ *RIGHT Ian Appleyard replaced his SS 100 with an XK120 (NUB 120). It was to prove one of the most successful combinations of car and driver the world of rallying has ever known.*

♦ JAGUAR XK120 ♦
DROPHEAD COUPE

BODY STYLE(s): Two Seater Convertible with folding hood.
ENGINE: XK Twin overhead cam 6 cyl, 3442 cc
MAX POWER: 190 bhp
TIME: 0–60 9.5 secs
MAX SPEED: 119.5 mph
QUANTITY MADE: 294 (rhd)   1471 (lhd)
PRICE: £1660
ANNOUNCEMENT DATE: March 1951
IN PRODUCTION: 1951–1954

practical for everyday use. Since the 120's were coming to the end of their production lives, the Dropheads, most of which, like the other models, were exported, were made in fewer numbers. Some 7,612 Roadsters, 2,678 Fixed Heads and 1,765 Dropheads were built before they were discontinued in late 1954, to be replaced by the XK140's. The 140 differed in a number of minor, though often important, ways from the 120, but the concept remained essentially the same. The basic shape, chassis, suspension and XK power-unit were all similar.

The changes were made in response to demand and were intended to be improvements. In retrospect, though, many have a fondness for the original 120's and feel that with the 140's the XK's went 'soft'. That the cosmetic changes were retrograde most people agree; on the other hand, many feel that the mechanical changes make the 140's more pleasant to drive.

There were a number of external modifications. The rather delicate front bumpers and rear overriders gave way to American demands for

■ *ABOVE AND RIGHT In October, 1954, the XK120 was replaced by the evolutionary XK140. All three models were again offered. The XK140 Drophead, like all the 140's had external trim differences, including the rather unsightly over-heavy bumpers. In common with the Fixed Head model, it benefited from the addition of two small rear seats.*

◆ J A G U A R   X K 1 4 0 ◆
D R O P H E A D   C O U P E

BODY STYLE(s): 2+2 Convertible
  with folding hood
ENGINE: XK Twin overhead cam
  6 cyl, 3442 cc
MAX POWER: 190 bhp
TIME: 0–60 11 secs
MAX SPEED: 129.2 mph
QUANTITY MADE: 479 (rhd)   2310 (lhd)
PRICE: £1664
ANNOUNCEMENT DATE: Oct 1954
IN PRODUCTION: 1954–1957

◆ C O L O U R   S C H E M E S   F O R   X K 1 4 0 ◆

COACHWORK	INTERIOR			TOP	
	OPEN TWO-SEATER	FIXED HEAD COUPÉ	DROPHEAD COUPÉ	OPEN TWO-SEATER	DROPHEAD COUPÉ
Black	Red, Biscuit and Red two-tone	Red, Tan, Grey Biscuit	Red, Tan, Grey Biscuit	Black	Black, Sand
Birch Grey	Red, Biscuit and Red two-tone	Red, Blue, Grey	Red, Grey, Pale Blue	French Grey, Black	French Grey, Black
Pastel Green	Suede Green	Suede Green	Suede Green, Grey	Fawn, Black	Fawn, Black
Pearl Grey	Red, Blue, Grey	Red, Blue, Grey	Red, Blue, Grey	Blue, Black, French Grey	Blue, Black French Grey
Pacific Blue	Blue, Grey	Blue, Grey	Blue, Grey	Blue, Black	Blue, Black
British Racing Green	Tan, Suede Green	Tan, Suede Green	Tan, Suede Green	Gunmetal, Black	Gunmetal, Black
Dove Grey	Tan, Biscuit	Tan, Biscuit	Tan Biscuit	Fawn, Sand, Black	Fawn, Sand, Black
Suede Green	Suede Green	Suede Green	Suede Green	French Grey, Black	French Grey, Black
Red	Red, Biscuit and Red two-tone	Red	Red	Fawn, Black	Fawn, Black
Lavender Grey	Red, Suede Green, Pale Blue	Red, Suede Green	Red, Suede Green, Pale Blue	Fawn, Black	Fawn, Black
Battleship Grey	Red, Biscuit and Red two-tone	Red, Grey	Red, Grey, Biscuit	Gunmetal, Black	Gunmetal, Black
Cream	Red, Biscuit and Red two-tone	Red	Red, Pale Blue	Fawn, Black, Blue	Fawn, Black, Blue
Pastel Blue	Light and Dark Blue two-tone, Blue	Light Blue	Light Blue	French Grey, Black, Blue	French Grey, Black, Blue
Maroon	Red, Biscuit	Red, Biscuit	Red, Biscuit	Black, Sand	Black, Sand

something sturdier to protect the cars against the large and heavy products of Detroit! The 120's grille, which was expensive to make, was replaced by a heavier-looking cast item. Chrome trim strips appeared on the bonnet and bootlid, the latter now three-quarters its former length and lockable. The number plate was now carried on the fixed panel below the bootlid and the rear lights were slightly changed in size and style. The 'tripod' headlamps were replaced by better ones with a small 'J' badge in the middle, and flashing indicator lights appeared on the front wings.

Mechanically, the recirculating-ball steering of the 120's was superseded by rack and pinion, which made the steering a lot lighter. Universal joints in the column allowed the steering wheel to be set less upright, making driving more comfortable. The engines were moved three inches forward, ostensibly to improve legroom, but as a bonus improving the front-to-rear weight ratio and handling. The former Special Equipment 190-bhp engines were now fitted as standard, as were uprated torsion bars and telescopic rear shock absorbers.

All three body styles were again offered and the Drophead and Fixed Head models were altered to include two very small rear seats for children or an occasional adult. The microscopic rear window of the Drophead was enlarged and the Fixed Head was considerably altered. The whole interior compartment was increased in size by moving the base of the windscreen

forward and extending the roof six inches rearward. Unlike the other models, the XK140 Fixed Head had footwells which extended alongside the engine, thereby increasing interior space even more.

Cruising ability was enhanced by the option of overdrive on the 140's and a little later automatic transmission could be specified. The latter was popular in the United States, where the customers now expected it. Exports continued to thrive and the XK's enjoyed something of a cult status in the USA. Before the war fewer than 10 per cent of the XK's that were built had been exported; by 1951 the figure had risen to 80 per cent. Together with MG, Jaguar had become Great Britain's most successful dollar-earner.

The 140's made many friends and, although the 120 is remembered as

■ *LEFT, TOP AND BOTTOM The XK140 Fixed Head was the most changed of the trio. With footwells extended to improve footroom and the roofline also extended both forwards and rearwards, the interior was considerably more roomy.*

■ *ABOVE In body style the XK140 Roadster was the least changed, but like all the XK140's it was fitted with an uprated engine, rack and pinion steering and various other mechanical improvements.*

◆ JAGUAR XK140 ◆
FIXED HEAD COUPE

BODY STYLE(s): Closed 2+2 Seater Coupe
ENGINE: XK Twin overhead cam
    6 cyl, 3442 cc
MAX POWER: 190 bhp
TIME: 0–60 11 secs
MAX SPEED: 129.2 mph
QUANTITY MADE: 843 (rhd)   1965 (lhd)
PRICE: £1616
ANNOUNCEMENT DATE: Oct 1954
IN PRODUCTION: 1954–1957

the 'classic', they have a devoted band of followers. One distinguished former owner commented favourably years later on those oft-criticized bumpers. Apparently an Edinburgh Corporation bus hit his XK140 Fixed Head up the back as a result of sheet ice. The XK's reversing light was a millimetre out of true as a consequence. The bus fared a little worse. Its whole front end was stoved in!

Between 1954 and 1957, 2,808 Fixed Heads and 2,789 Dropheads left the factory. The Roadsters were the most plentiful with 3,354 constructed; but only 73 were right-hand drive cars and of those only 47 remained in Great Britain. Right-hand drive versions of the Fixed Heads and Dropheads numbered 843 and 479 respectively.

The fabulous XKSS was created in the latter part of 1956 by which time the factory had already begun, in a very limited way, to build production versions of the racing D-types (see Chapter 5) for private buyers who wished to go motor racing. Extraordinary though it now sounds, when such cars are among the most valuable and revered in the world, Jaguar had more shells than they could sell. Thus was born the idea of making the remainder into more civilized road cars, ones with the additional advantage of allowing US customers to enter the production car classes in their country.

Unfortunately, only 16 left the factory before a calamity destroyed the remaining cars and the vital jigs. In February 1957, near-disaster struck the company when fire broke out at the Browns Lane factory. Luckily it was brought under control and the damage minimized. Nevertheless, considerable damage was done and many cars spoiled. All those affected

■ RIGHT The fabulous and very rare XKSS was a roadgoing, more civilized, version of the sports racing production D-type. Important jigs were lost in the factory fire after only 16 models had been made and no more were manufactured.

■ BELOW The XK150 Drophead Coupe, like its sister models, did not have the dramatic rise and fall of the wing line so characteristic of earlier models, but it had the immense benefit of race proved disc brakes and a range of more powerful engines.

♦ JAGUAR XKSS ♦

BODY STYLE(s): Refined version of D-type
Two Seater Sports Racing Car
ENGINE: XK Twin overhead cam
6 cyl, 3442 cc
MAX POWER: 250 bhp
TIME: 0–60 5.2 secs
MAX SPEED: 149 mph
QUANTITY MADE: 16 (plus 2 D-types
converted later by factory)
PRICE: £3878
ANNOUNCEMENT DATE: Jan 1957
IN PRODUCTION: 1957

were scrapped and with a Herculean effort by men, management and suppliers, production was restarted within a couple of days. In spite of this setback, 1957 proved to be another record year. Nothing, it seemed, could stop Lyons' company. He himself was now Sir William Lyons, having been knighted the previous year.

Whilst the XK's were unquestionably good cars, their brakes had always given faster drivers cause for concern. In competition those problems were, of course, magnified. In association with Dunlop, Jaguar had successfully developed the disc brake for racing, and given their obvious advantages, it was logical that they should be fitted to the Jaguar production sports cars. In 1957 this happened and the new XK150's superseded the 140's.

The new cars differed from the 140's more than the 140's had from the 120's. The concept again remained the same, with a very similar chassis and method of body construction, but the body was somewhat different. Character was sacrificed to modernization. Gone was the evocative rise and fall of the wing line. In came the new one-piece windscreen. With the adoption of thinner doors, the interior space was increased. A section added

---

♦ J A G U A R ♦
X K 1 4 0   O P E N

BODY STYLE(s): Open Two Seater Roadster
ENGINE: XK Twin overhead cam
   6 cyl, 3442 cc
MAX POWER: 190 bhp
TIME: 0–60 8.4 secs (S.E. model)
MAX SPEED: 121.1 mph (S.E. model)
QUANTITY MADE: 73 (rhd – 47 U.K. market)
   3281 (lhd)
PRICE: £1598
ANNOUNCEMENT DATE: Oct 1954
IN PRODUCTION: 1954–1957

◆ JAGUAR XK150 ◆
FIXED HEAD COUPE
& DROPHEAD COUPE

BODY STYLE(s): Closed & Convertible 2+2
ENGINE: XK Twin overhead cam
3442 & 3781 cc
MAX POWER: 190 bhp (3442 cc)
210 bhp (3442 cc S.E. model)
250 bhp (3442 cc 'S' model)
220 bhp (3781 cc)
265 bhp (3781 cc 'S' model)
TIME: 0–60 8.5 secs (3442 cc S.E.)
7.8 secs (3442 cc 'S') 7.6 secs (3781 cc 'S')
MAX SPEED: 123.7 mph (3442 cc S.E.)
132 mph (3442 cc 'S')
136.3 mph (3781 cc 'S')
QUANTITY MADE: Fixed Head Coupe
3445 (3442 cc & S.E.) 199 (3442 cc 'S')
656 (3781 cc & S.E.) 150 (3781 cc 'S')
Drophead Coupe 1903 (3442 cc & S.E.)
104 (3442 cc 'S') 586 (3781 & S.E.)
89 (3781 cc 'S')
PRICE: Fixed Head Coupe £1763 (3442 cc)
£1940 (3442 cc S.E.) £2065 (3442 cc 'S')
£2065 (3781 cc) £2175 (3781 cc 'S')
Drophead Coupe £1793 (3442 cc)
£1940 (3442 cc S.E.) £2093 (3442 cc 'S')
£1970 (3781 cc) £2204 (3781 cc 'S')
ANNOUNCEMENT DATE: May 1957
(FHC & DHC 3442 cc & S.E.)
Feb 1959 (FHC & DHC 3442 cc 'S')
Oct 1959
(FHC & DHC 3781 cc & 3781 cc 'S')
IN PRODUCTION: 1957–1960
(DHC 3442 cc & S.E.)
1957–1961 (FHC 3442 cc & S.E.)
1959–1960
(DHC 3442 cc 'S', 3781 cc & 3781 cc 'S')
1959–1961
(FHC 3442 cc 'S', 3781 cc & 3781 cc 'S')

The later XK's rarely enjoyed the spectacular success of the earlier 120's simply because racing was becoming ever more sophisticated. However, there were notable exceptions to this generalization. Two amateurs took a virtually standard XK140 FHC to Le Mans and were extremely unlucky to be disqualified while in 11th place, having seen off the challenge of a Mercedes-Benz 300SL. Ian Appleyard occasionally rallied a similar model. Bobbie Parks rallied a 140 and Ronnie Adams, better known for his success with the big saloons, entered a 140 Roadster in the 1956 RAC Rally.

In the United States, Chuck Wallace took the 1955 SCCA C-Production class championship in his 140 and in Great Britain a former Daimler apprentice, young David Hobbs (who is still racing in the United States today) drove furiously and effectively in a 140 FHC fitted with his father's Hobbs Mechamatic transmission. Later the car was rebodied as a Fixed Head and, like many historic XK's, is campaigned enthusiastically today, this one in Austria.

Jack Lambert, Don Parker, Don Smith and Warren Pearce all raced 150's and the rally pairing, Haddon and Vivien, who had tasted success with their 120, took the GT Class and 10th overall in the 1960 Tulip Rally.

■ *TOP The XK150, seen here in Drophead form, was more radically modified than its predecessor the 140 had been, although the separate, strong, box-section chassis was changed only in detail.*

■ *LEFT All the XK150's, including the Fixed Head seen here, benefited from a one-piece windscreen, more slender doors (which improved interior width) and a wider bonnet (which gave better engine access).*

to the middle of the bonnet improved engine accessibility without the cost of expensive new tooling. The old-fashioned interior walnut gave way to aluminium and later to leather.

The 140's had been more sophisticated than the 120's, and the 150's were another step in that direction. The XK was, as the market demanded, becoming more of a sporting, touring car than a downright sports car. This is not to say that the 150's did not have performance. Special Equipment models were fitted with the B-type head, which increased power from 190 bhp to 210 bhp and gave considerably improved torque. In spite of this,

♦ JAGUAR XK150 ♦
OPEN TWO SEATER

BODY STYLE(s): Open Two Seater Roadster
ENGINE: XK Twin overhead cam 6 cyl,
3442 & 3781 cc
MAX POWER: As XK150 FHC & DHC
TIME: 0–60 7.3 secs (3442 cc 'S')
MAX SPEED: 136 mph (3442 cc 'S')
QUANTITY MADE: 1297 (3442 cc & S.E.)
888 (3442 cc 'S') 42 (3781 cc & S.E.)
36 (3781 cc 'S')
PRICE: £1666 (3442 cc) £2065 (3442 cc 'S')
£2065 (3781 cc) £2176 (3781 cc 'S')
ANNOUNCEMENT DATE: March 1958
(3442 cc, S.E. & 'S')
Oct 1959 (3781 cc & 'S')
IN PRODUCTION: 1958–1960
(3442 cc, S.E., 'S')
1959–1960 (3781 cc & 'S')

certain competitors, notably in the United States, were catching up with the XK's in terms of straight acceleration. However, when it came to cornering and, now particularly, stopping, to say nothing of value for money, the XK150's were still in a league of their own. Initially, only the Fixed Head and Drophead models were made available, but early in 1958 the familiar Roadster joined the ranks. The 'S' version was offered at the same time and 'S' versions of the other 150 models became available later.

Harry Weslake, again working his magic on the cylinder heads, produced what was known as 'the straight port head'. With three large SU carburettors, a lightened flywheel and stronger clutch, the 'S' engine produced 250 bhp, again with increased torque. As ever (this was always of paramount importance to Jaguar engineers) the car was smooth, docile and flexible. During development the testers always concentrated on top-gear performance even more than that through the gears. Thus Jaguars, justifiably famous for their performance, were equally renowned for their gentle, quiet, effortless qualities.

Mindful of several manufacturers who were dropping ever larger V8 engines into their sporting cars, Jaguar replied with an enlarged 3.8 litre version of the trusty XK unit. This new engine could be had with the B-type head or the 'S' straight port head and these were additional models rather

■ *LEFT* Donald Campbell had his XK150 Fixed Head painted to match his record-breaking power boat, Bluebird.

■ *ABOVE AND RIGHT* Shortly after the introduction of the Fixed and Drophead XK150's, a Roadster version joined the range. It shared the various mechanical improvements and styling changes. The ultimate 3.8 'S' version was a very quick car and produced some 265 bhp.

Over the years a number of well-known styling houses and coachbuilders produced ideas for body styles mounted on Jaguar chassis. Before the war several continental firms offered rather strange creations on SS Jaguar chassis and the Coventry agent, S.H. Newsome, had two drophead bodies built on '100' chassis. The XK's came in for the same treatment. A Mr Park of Kew built his attempt at a Fixed Head 120 before the factory itself did, but it had nothing of the style of the official XK120 FHC. Abbot built an ugly four-seater drophead by extending the roofline rearwards. Pininfarina built a body in the style of the current Italian exotica and Oblin's offering also reminds one of Ferraris. Indeed, most of these models reflected the 'house' style and every commentator has always felt that Lyons' own styling was rarely approached, let alone matched. Ghia had two attempts at alternatives on the XK140 chassis, but the most interesting 140 'special' was one designed by the famous American-based French industrial designer, Raymond Loewy. Very modern for its year, it now looks very ugly, not least because of the brace of trumpet horns mounted atop the front wings! Interesting features included a sloping nose and a wrap-around, one-piece rear window. Michelotti designed a most pleasing body for a crashed D-type, and Bertone, one of the few designers Lyons ever encouraged and assisted (he may even have commissioned him), produced his own version of the XK150 (shown above).

than replacements. Thus, with three body styles and four mechanical specifications listed, no fewer than 12 different XK150's were being produced.

The 3.8 engine in standard form produced 220 bhp and the ultimate 3.8 litre 'S' yielded a very impressive 265 bhp, with equally impressive torque characteristics. The latter version gave the 150 a top speed of 136 mph. It could reach 60 mph in just 7.6 seconds, while the standing quarter-mile took only 16 seconds.

The XK150's were, therefore, very fast cars with superb braking. There was no denying, however, that the design dated back to the late forties and that the chassis was now somewhat old-fashioned. The body shape was not so aerodynamically efficient as was now desirable. Something completely new was therefore required to put Jaguar once more several steps ahead of the opposition. When this new sports car arrived on the scene in 1961 it caused as big a sensation as the XK120 had back in 1948.

■ RIGHT The XK150's, including the Roadster model seen here, remained popular but, more than a decade having passed since the concept was originally seen, they were becoming a little dated, at least by Jaguar standards. Could Jaguar now apply the lessons learned from the racing D types to a new road car?

CHAPTER FOUR

THE SPORTING SEDANS

*W*hile the racing cars brought fame and
the sports cars chic, it was the production
of the saloons (sedans), which ensured a sound
financial base for the company.

The Jaguar company's post-war saloons consisted of the resurrected Mark IV's (as they have become known) and the Mark V's, and excellent cars though these were, their day was over. Something new was required, not only to maintain interest, but also to take another step up the prestige ladder. Furthermore, with supplies of steel in the post-war 'ration' economy dependent on export success, the company needed a car designed to make inroads into the dollar market. The XK engine had been designed with greater technical merit in mind, as had the Mark V's new chassis and independent front suspension. What they needed was packaging in a modern new body. The massive, but stylish, Mark VII was the result and it was another great Lyons success.

■ *The Mark VII saloon was launched at Earl's Court, London, in 1950 and its success was immediate. The Mark VII, together with the XK120 sports car, did much to establish the prestige of British automotive engineering in the 1950s and earned valuable American dollars for the British exchequer.*

◆ J A G U A R ◆
MARK VII
SALOON

BODY STYLE(s): Large Five/Six Seater,
Four Door Saloon
ENGINE: XK Twin overhead cam
6 cyl, 3442 cc
MAX POWER: 160 bhp
TIME: 0–60 13.7 secs
MAX SPEED: 101 mph
QUANTITY MADE: 12,755 (rhd) 8184 (lhd)
PRICE: £1276
ANNOUNCEMENT DATE: Oct 1950
IN PRODUCTION: 1951–1954

■ The Mark VII was large by British
standards, because it was designed very
much with the United States market in mind.
Everywhere its modern, but graceful, body
seemed to meet acclaim.

■ The Mark VII, powered by the brilliant twin overhead cam XK engine already made famous by the XK120, had a very respectable performance for its size and weight. The flagship of the Jaguar company, it could achieve the magic 100 mph while carrying five people.

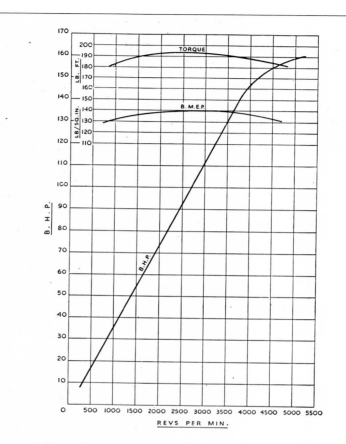

The graph above shows the power curve of the famous Jaguar XK engine. To the left is a general view of the engine showing the twin carburetters. Below is a partially sectioned drawing which shows the arrangement of the drive for the twin over-head camshafts.

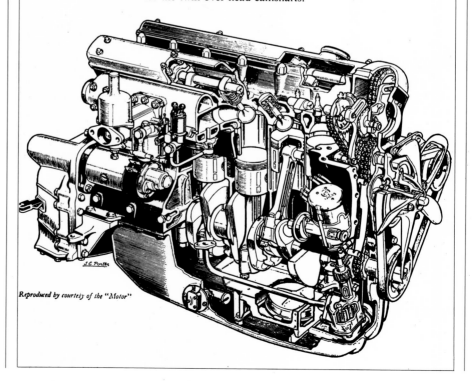

Reproduced by courtesy of the "Motor"

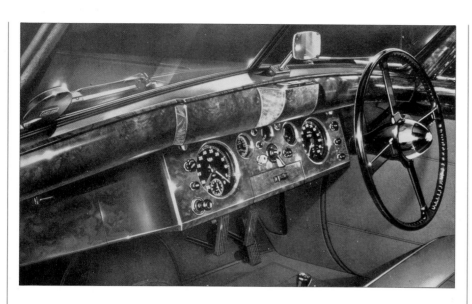

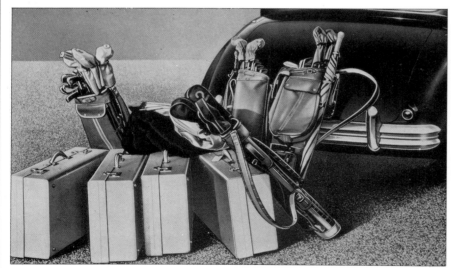

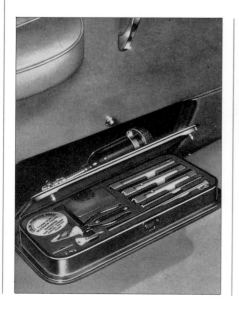

■ Not only could the Mark VII carry five people at virtually unheard-of speeds, it did in great comfort. It also accommodated copious amounts of luggage and retained pre-war levels of opulence, with splendid touches of detail like the tool trays mounted in the doors.

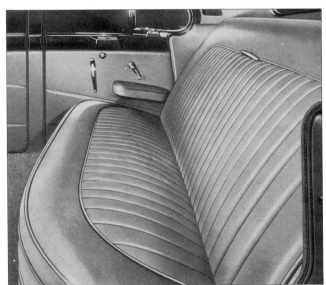

In spite of its large size and weight, the new car, launched at the 1950 Earl's Court Motor Show, was capable of the magic 100 mph and could reach 60 mph from rest in just over 12 seconds. The large body gave generous space and comfort for six passengers and the 17 cubic feet of boot space looked after their luggage requirements. There was also good visibility all round. Girling autostatic hydraulic brakes were adopted and were said to break fresh ground in having two 'trailing' shoes in the front drums. Advertisements boasted of the 'famous XK120 engine', though that model had been almost an afterthought.

The press was won over. Comments included, 'A world beater . . . if ever there was one' (*Daily Mail*), 'Well over 100 miles per hour and phenomenal acceleration' (*Daily Telegraph*) and 'A sleek, streamlined six-seater with every luxury fitment possible' (*Sporting Life*). The *Times* felt that the Mark VII 'achieved an objective which previously eluded British manufacturers . . . unmistakably British yet with modern lines'.

The car was also a great success in the United States and it was not long before automatic transmission was offered and, a little later, the option of overdrive. Exports boomed and Jaguar struggled to meet demand. The company was outgrowing the old munitions factory at Swallow Road, even though new extensions and shops had increased the site to about 15 times its original size. Lyons pulled off another coup when he managed, with assistance from the Ministry of Supply, to acquire Daimler's wartime shadow factory. The new premises of no less than one million square feet, nearly double their existing buildings, gave Jaguar the scope for major expansion.

Big though the Mark VII was, it was still a genuinely sporting car and it proved it in rallying and racing. At the beginning of 1952 the car finished in fourth and sixth positions on the gruelling Monte Carlo Rally and in April

♦JAGUAR♦
MARK VII M SALOON

BODY STYLE(s): Large Five/Six
    Seater Saloon
ENGINE: XK Twin overhead cam
    6 cyl, 3442 cc
MAX POWER: 190 bhp
TIME: 0–60 14.1 secs
MAX SPEED: 104.3 mph
QUANTITY MADE: 10,061
PRICE: £1616
ANNOUNCEMENT DATE: Oct 1954
IN PRODUCTION: 1954–1957

■ *Large and luxurious the Mark VII's might have been, but they were still sporting cars and a number of models gained international success in European rallies, including the Monte Carlo Rally.*

Ian Appleyard took a Mark VII to second place in the Tulip Rally. A month later the factory entered a Mark VII for the newly created Production Touring Car Race. The driver, Stirling Moss, gained an impressive victory, the beginning of Jaguar's domination of that event at Silverstone for the next 10 years.

The year 1953 saw Appleyard finish second on the Monte with a Mark VII, Scott win his class in the R.A.C. Rally and Appleyard win the Tulip Rally. Moss won at Silverstone again, though in 1954 he could manage only third place after trouble with a jammed starter. However, Jaguar honour was upheld by Appleyard and Rolt, who occupied the two higher positions in Jaguar-entered Mark VII's, thereby enabling the company to take the team prize.

In 1954 the Mark VII was improved by the introduction of the Mark VIIM. This model had the XK140 190-bhp engine and a gearbox with closer ratios. With springs and dampers more suited to fast driving, it was described by one magazine as 'exceptional'. In appearance it was little changed. The spotlamps, formerly let into the wings directly below the headlamps, were attached to the bumper valances, their former position being filled by small circular grilles. The semaphore indicators were deleted and flasher lamps appeared on the front wings.

■ *It was not only in rallying that the Mark VII's showed their mettle. Young Stirling Moss and others took the large saloons to many victories on the race tracks, thus demonstrating their straight-line performance and good roadholding.*

♦**JAGUAR**♦
2.4 SALOON

BODY STYLE(s): Compact Four Door Saloon
ENGINE: XK Twin overhead cam
    6 cyl, 2483 cc
MAX POWER: 112 bhp
TIME: 0–60 14.4 secs
MAX SPEED: 101.5 mph
QUANTITY MADE: 19,400
PRICE: £1344
ANNOUNCEMENT DATE: Sept 1955
IN PRODUCTION: 1955–1959

The XK sports cars and these big saloons, designed very much for the United States, where such large cars were the norm, sold extremely well. But there remained a gap in the range. There was room for a small, sporting, luxury saloon which would be popular on the narrower roads of Europe and might also appeal to a new market in the United States as a sporting compact.

The small saloon announced in 1955 marked a new technical approach by Jaguar. Instead of having a separate body and chassis, the new 2.4 saved weight by having a body of stressed unitary construction. The legendary designer, Sir Alec Issigonis (creator of the Mini), had used such a construction before the war for his racing car known as the Lightweight Special. Heynes and Hassan had themselves played with such construction techniques during the war while building little jeeps. The saloon was not without its problems, which required the expert attention of Bob Knight, an engineer who had joined the company in the forties. Knight was to earn a unique reputation for refining cars and he learned a great deal while improving the 2.4. He skilfully used different types and hardnesses of rubber to mount items and so reduce noise.

The new car was known as the 2.4 because it had a 2.4-litre version of the XK engine. Jaguar had played around with the original four-cylinder XK100 engine for several years and considered it for this model. However, it could never be made sufficiently quiet and smooth and so a short-stroke version of the useful 3.4 was built for the new car. Jaguar was keen to retain its reputation for refinement and flexibility and there were fears that the four-cylinder, with its inherent imbalance, might prove troublesome by transmitting vibrations to the unitary construction body. The suspension was a departure from normal Jaguar practice. A separate rubber-mounted front sub-frame carried the coil spring and wishbone arrangement. The back axle was supported by trailing arms and cantilever semi-elliptic springs. Curiously, the rear track was narrower than the front, so that high-speed stability was not as good as it might have been.

In the competition world, three Mark VII's driven by Adams, Vard and Appleyard took the Charles Faroux Team Trophy at the 1955 Monte Carlo

■ *By the mid-1950s Jaguar had a world-beating sports car and a successful, large, luxury saloon in the range, but still needed a 'volume' car to boost production and fill a gap in the line-up. The 2.4 saloon was that model.*

■ *In 1956 the Mark VIII appeared, replacing the Mark VII, from which it differed only in details. The most noticeable innovations were the one-piece windscreen, the cutaway spats, the chrome grille surround and the two-tone colour scheme.*

◆**JAGUAR**◆
MARK VIII SALOON

BODY STYLE(s): Large Five/Six
  Seater Saloon
ENGINE: XK Twin overhead cam
  6 cyl, 3442 cc
MAX POWER: 210 bhp
TIME: 0–60 11.6 secs
MAX SPEED: 106.5 mph
QUANTITY MADE: 6212
PRICE: £1830
ANNOUNCEMENT DATE: Oct 1956
IN PRODUCTION: 1956–1959

JAGUAR AND THE SUEZ CRISIS

*D*uring the Suez crisis British motorists were limited to 10 gallons of petrol per month. With a fuel consumption of 23 mpg when driven very gently, the Mark VII could thus do only just over 200 miles a month.
Louis Giron and Bowman's Garage of Weybridge developed a modification to improve consumption. The standard twin SU carburettors were supplemented by a third of smaller choke diameter. A slip-linkage opened the single throttle first and greater pressure opened the main throttles when needed. A calibrated restrictor venturi, which limited the gas speed through the carburettor choke, was situated in the subsidiary manifold. Performance was obviously reduced, but useful savings seem to have been achieved. A prototype was able to record 34 – 38 mpg at 30 – 35 mph, and cruising 45 – 55 mph gave 25 – 30 mpg.

Rally and a similar car again won its class in the R.A.C. Rally. In May a new factory line-up of Mike Hawthorn, Jimmy Stewart (brother of the future world champion, Jackie) and Desmond Titterington finished in the first three places in the annual Silverstone saloon car race.

At the same event in 1956 three of the new 2.4's were entered by the factory. Two of them, however, had problems and Duncan Hamilton could finish only third. Luckily Jaguar had entered a couple of Mark VII's just in case. Bueb, in one, did an excellent job keeping Ken Wharton in an Austin Westminster at bay and just managed to keep ahead and win for the Coventry marque. The Monte Carlo Rally of that year saw a splendid victory for Adams, Bigger and Johnston, who won in their Mark VII after years of trying.

In October 1956 the big Mark VII was updated in a number of minor ways and renamed the Mark VIII. The new car was a little quicker as a result of its B-type cylinder head and twin exhaust system. A switch was added to the dashboard whereby the driver could, on automatic transmission models, choose and hold a particular gear as desired. Otherwise the car remained mechanically little changed. The appearance was updated in various subtle ways. A chrome strip was added to the body sides, tracing the wing line and breaking up the rather plain, slab slides; a two-tone colour scheme was

introduced (the dividing line being the chrome beading); the archaic two-piece split windscreen was superseded by a more pleasing single item; the radiator acquired a more prominent appearance as a result of a new, deeper chrome surround; and the external updating was completed by giving the rear wheel spats a small cutaway, again lessening the effect of bulk.

The famous leaping Jaguar mascot, an optional extra in the past, was added to the Mark VIII's bonnet top and veneered, fold-down picnic tables on the rear of the front seats provided a new touch of luxury. These front seats, incidentally, were of a single-bench type in the automatic models, but individual in the comparatively rare manual transmission models.

Soon after the factory fire, the company rolled out an addition to the 'compact' range. The 3.4-litre had been expected for some time, and in 1957 it officially appeared. The car was re-engineered to take the larger, heavier and more powerful power plant. A new rear axle with modified Panhard rod mounting was adopted, the suspension uprated and the engine mountings altered. A larger clutch and radiator block were also incorporated. With its B-type 3,442-cc engine, fitted with twin SU HD6 carburettors and capable of producing 210 bhp, the 3.4 saloon was a 120-mph car. The ability to reach 60 mph in 9.1 seconds from standstill was impressive and the price, as ever, was remarkable at just £1,672.

The new model was easily recognizable by its larger grille with more slender slats. The cutaway spats, too, allowed rather more of the rear wheels to be seen, thus improving the appearance considerably. Those trying to keep up with this rapid sports saloon would notice that the 3.4 also had twin exhaust pipes.

Following the fire, the small overstretched team of engineers needed to concentrate on developing production cars. The company announced in October, therefore, that it was pulling out of motor racing, though it would continue to assist privateers to some extent. Several such enthusiasts entered 3.4's for the annual Silverstone touring car race and their success surprised no one. Hawthorn led over the line, followed by Hamilton and Bueb.

The 2.4 acquired its larger brother's wider grille in September 1957 and disc brakes, which were much-needed, particularly by the racing drivers,

---

♦ **J A G U A R** ♦
3.4 SALOON

BODY STYLE(s): Compact Four Door Saloon
ENGINE: XK Twin overhead cam
   6 cyl, 3442 cc
MAX POWER: 210 bhp
TIME: 0–60 9.1 secs
MAX SPEED: 120 mph
QUANTITY MADE: 17,340
PRICE: £1672
ANNOUNCEMENT DATE: March 1957
IN PRODUCTION: 1957–1959

■ *The 3.4 saloon, which joined its smaller sister in 1957, had the more usual 3.4-litre engine, which gave it very lively performance for the period. The model was a great favourite of family men who yearned for a sporting car but for one reason or another could no longer justify an XK to their wives!*

were offered as an option on both models from the start of 1958. At the Motor Show that year the Mark VII was again revised and became the final version of this concept, the Mark IX.

For some time several racing teams, including the famous Lister sports racing cars, had used XK engines bored out to 3.8 litres. With the advent of the Mark IX, Jaguar adopted the 3.8 and it gave a very lively performance to this grossly heavy car. The taxing job of stopping such a machine was catered for by fitting the new disc brakes. A belated addition to the specification was power steering, which must have been sorely missed on its predecessors, particularly in the United States, where it had been used for some while. Thus the large Jaguars, which remained visually unchanged, were brought up to date, although something rather newer, without a

◆ THE MARK IX SALOON ◆

ENGINE: Special six cylinder 3.8 litre Jaguar engine. 70° twin overhead high lift camshafts driven by a two stage roller chain. 87 mm bore × 106 mm stroke. 3781 cc developing 120 bhp. Compression ratio 8:1. High grade chrome iron cylinder block, cooling by pump with by-pass thermostat control. Cylinder head of high tensile aluminium alloy with hemispherical combustion chambers developed from "C" and "D" type racing heads. Aluminium alloy pistons. Steel connecting rods. Forced lubrication throughout by submerged pump with full-flow filter. Twin S.U. type H.D.6 horizontal carburettors with electrically controlled automatic choke. 2¾ ins diameter counterweighted crankshaft carried in seven large steel backed precision bearings. Twin exhaust system. This engine has been specially developed to produce exceptionally high torque in the lower and middle speed ranges.

FRAME: Straight plane steel box section frame of immense strength; torsional rigidity ensured by large box section cross members.

TRANSMISSION: (A) Manually operated gearbox. Four-speed single helical synchromesh gearbox. Gear change lever on floor between front seats. Gear ratios: Top, 4.27; 3rd, 5.16; 2nd, 7.47; 1st, 12.73; Rev., 12.73. (B) Manually operated gearbox with overdrive. Gear ratios: Overdrive, 3.54; Top, 4.55; 3rd, 5.50; 2nd, 7.96; 1st, 13.56; Rev., 13.56. (C) Borg Warner Automatic Transmission with driver controlled intermediate gear. Gear ratios: Low range from 21.2 to 9.86; intermediate range from 13.2 to 6.14; Top (direct drive), 4.27 to 1.

SUSPENSION: Independent front suspension incorporating transverse wishbones, long torsion bars and telescopic shock absorbers. Rear suspension by long silico-manganese steel half elliptic springs controlled by telescopic shock-absorbers.

CLUTCH: Special heavy duty 10″ single dry plate clutch with hydraulic operation.

BRAKES: Dunlop disc brakes with servo assistance and special quickly detachable pads.

STEERING: Burman power-assisted re-circulating ball-type steering. Power assistance is by hydraulic pressure from a pump driven from the rear of the dynamo. Number of turns from lock to lock, 3½. 18″ adjustable steering wheel. Left or right hand steering optional.

WHEELS AND TYRES: Pressed steel bolt-on disc wheels with wide base rims fitted with Embellishers and Dunlop 6.70 × 16 ins. Road Speed tyres.

FUEL SUPPLY: Twin S.U. electric fuel pumps. Fuel capacity 17 imperial gallons in two separate tanks of nine and eight gallons, with turn-over switch on instrument panel.

ELECTRICAL EQUIPMENT, INSTRUMENTS AND FITTINGS: Lucas 12-volt system. Twin 6-volt batteries giving 64 amp/hour at 10-hour rate, with current voltage control. Flush fitting headlamps and wing lamps, twin adjustable fog lamps, integral stop/tail lamps with built-in reflectors, reverse lamp, self-cancelling flashing direction indicators with warning light, panel lights, door-operated and manually controlled interior lights, twin blended note horns, twin blade two-speed screen wipers, three cigar lighters, starter motor, vacuum and centrifugal automatic ignition advance, oil coil ignition, 5 ins diameter 120 mph speedometer, 5 ins diameter revolution counter, ammeter, oil pressure gauge, water thermometer gauge, fuel gauge, electric clock, windscreen washers.

HEATER AND AIR CONDITIONING: Built-in heater with controlled warm air flow and incorporating windscreen de-frosters. Two speed booster fan.

BODY AND APPOINTMENTS: All steel full five or six seater with sliding roof. Four doors. Ventilating windows front and rear. Special security locks to rear doors for child safety. Bench type front seat (automatic transmission model only) adjustable for reach; bucket seats on other models adjustable for height and reach. All seats luxuriously upholstered in highest quality fine-grain soft-tanned Vaumol leather over extra deep moulded Dunlopillo. Polished figured walnut instrument panel and interior garnishings. Two glove compartments, passengers' glove box fitted with lock. Sunvisors. Four ashtrays. Polished figured walnut flush folding occasional tables in rear compartment. Padded armrests all round and central fold-back armrest in rear and front compartments on bench seat model, rear compartment only on bucket seat model. Deep pile carpets upon ¼″ thick felt underlay. Additional nylon floor rug in rear. Boudoir clock and document cabinet fitted with lock in rear compartment (bench seat models only).

LUGGAGE ACCOMMODATION: The extraordinarily capacious luggage locker fitted with an interior light, enables four large suitcases, four sets of golf clubs, also rugs, holdalls, and other travelling sundries to be carried in its totally enclosed interior. The volume provided for the carrying of luggage is 17 cubic feet.

SPARE WHEEL: Fitted with Road Speed tyre and carried in luggage compartment with necessary tools for wheel changing.

TOOLS: A complete set of hand tools and small replacement items are carried in special flush fitting compartments concealed in the front doors.

EASY JACKING: Exterior jack slots conveniently placed, enable the car to be lifted with minimum effort by means of the jack provided.

PRINCIPAL DIMENSIONS: Wheelbase, 10 ft 0 ins; track front, 4 ft 8½ ins; track rear, 4 ft 10ins; overall length, 16 ft 4½ ins; overall width, 6 ft 1 in; overall height 5 ft 3 ins; ground clearance, 7½ ins; turning circle, 36 ft 0 ins; dry weight, 34½ cwt.

COLOUR SCHEMES: A wide range of colour schemes is available.

■ In 1958 the large saloon evolved a stage further with the introduction of the Mark IX. The major changes were the adoption of disc brakes and a 3.8-litre version of the XK engine. There were also changes to the grille. (Compare the illustrations above and inset right).

■ *LEFT* This description of the Mark IX saloon is taken from the factory brochure; the language is noticeably less extravagant than in pre-war specifications, perhaps reflecting a greater confidence.

◆ **JAGUAR** ◆
MARK IX SALOON

BODY STYLE(s): Large Five/Six
  Seater Saloon
ENGINE: XK Twin overhead cam
  6 cyl, 3781 cc
MAX POWER: 220 bhp
TIME: 0–60 11.3 secs
MAX SPEED: 114.3 mph
QUANTITY MADE: 10,009
PRICE: £1995
ANNOUNCEMENT DATE: Oct 1958
IN PRODUCTION: 1958–1961

chassis, came to be needed more and more urgently as time went by.

A British Touring Car Championship was organized for the first time in 1958 and Tommy Sopwith and Sir Gawaine Baillie teamed up to produce a number of wins. Hamilton, Hawthorn and Hansgen also managed wins during the year in 3.4's. In April, the Morley brothers took a 2.4 to a class win on the Tulip Rally and early in 1959 three 3.4's took the team prize on the Monte. Tragically, Mike Hawthorn was killed on the road in his 3.4, having just become the world champion of 1958. Sopwith retired and his Equipe Endeavour team was led by Ivor Bueb, with Sir Gawaine Baillie as number two. Their great rival, the John Coombs team, was led by Roy Salvadori. The three big races of the year finished in the order Bueb, Salvadori and Baillie.

Late in 1959, the 2.4 and 3.4 were superseded by considerably revised and much-improved versions known, not surprisingly, as Mark II's. (For this reason their predecessors have come to be known as Mark I's, though they were never officially named so.) The Mark II's were improved both visually and mechanically. More slender roof pillars and a larger, wrap-around rear window helped considerably, as did the new chrome side-window frames. The sidelights were removed from the front of the wings to the top, akin to those on the big saloons and XK's, but smaller. The new radiator grille sprouted a rib in the middle and the small grilles on either side gave way to spotlights. The dashboard layout was completely revised. The rev counter and speedometer were no longer grouped with the minor instruments and controls in a centre cluster; instead, the main instruments were mounted on either side of the steering column and the rest remained in the centre with a row of minor instruments above a row of switches. It was a layout that would gradually become universal throughout the range.

Mechanically, the most significant change was the adoption of a wider rear track. Three-and-a-quarter inches more may not sound a great deal,

---

♦ **JAGUAR MARK II** ♦
SALOON

BODY STYLE(s): Compact Four Door Saloon
ENGINE: XK Twin overhead cam
6 cyl, 2483, 3442 & 3781 cc
MAX POWER: 120 bhp (2.4) 210 bhp (3.4)
220 bhp (3.8)
TIME: 0–60 17.3 secs (2.4) 11.9 secs (3.4)
8.5 secs (3.8)
MAX SPEED: 96.3 mph (2.4)
119.9 mph (3.4)
125 mph (3.8)
QUANTITY MADE: 25,070 (2.4) 28,660 (3.4)
30,070 (3.8)
PRICE: £1534 (2.4) £1669 (3.4) £1779 (3.8)
ANNOUNCEMENT DATE: Oct 1959
IN PRODUCTION: 1959–1967

■ *The Mark II version of the small saloons was a great improvement on earlier models, both in appearance and mechanically. These cars continued to dominate saloon car racing, as the Mark VII's and 3.4's had done, and they provided some extremely entertaining dicing between some well-known Grand Prix drivers, including Graham Hill and Roy Salvadori.*

but it was all that could be accommodated without very costly re-designing of the rear bodywork and it certainly improved the handling, which was also assisted by alterations to the front suspension.

At the same time as the Mark II's were launched, the range was supplemented by the addition of a 3.8-litre model. This was a most exciting car and with its excellent power-to-weight ratio gave sparkling performance. The unit was fitted like the Mark IX with the B-type head and a power output of 220 bhp. With overdrive, the maximum speed was in the region of 125 mph and 60 mph could be reached in 8½ seconds. A Power-Lok limited slip differential allowed a driver to exploit this

DAIMLER

*I*n 1960 Jaguar was desperately short of space and needed to expand again. Thus it made sense to acquire the Daimler company, especially its factory in the Radford district of Coventry.

With these premises Jaguar inherited a diverse range of vehicles and a lineage as ancient as any in the British motor industry. The Daimler Motor Syndicate Ltd. was formed by Frederick Richard Simms in 1893 to sell engines produced by Gottlieb Daimler of Connstatt in Germany. Soon after production of Daimler-designed cars began in Coventry itself and in 1896 the Prince of Wales, later King Edward VII, was introduced to the Daimler car. That was the origin of an enduring association between the company and royalty. In 1910 Daimler merged with B.S.A. and during World War I began producing ambulances, lorries, staff cars and, for towing guns, cross-country tractors which were the prototypes of the first tanks. In 1931 Daimler took over the old-established firm of Lanchester. During World War II two 'Shadow Factories' were built and it was one of these, at Browns Lane, that Jaguar acquired just after the war.

After 1945, the range of buses and lorries flourished and a wide range of cars was manufactured. When Jaguar purchased Daimler in 1960 it continued the range of cars, including the Majestic Major, Limousine and SP250 sports car, and the commercial vehicles. Gradually, however, these models were replaced by Daimler versions of Jaguar models.

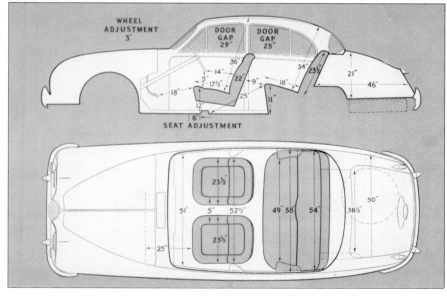

■ Coincident with the introduction of the Mark II models, Jaguar added a 3.8-litre version to the 2.4 and 3.4 variations. The 3.8 had electrifying performance and won high praise as a sporting compact. The illustration (TOP RIGHT) was used for a Jaguar company Christmas card of the period. The dash layout of the earlier models had the instruments grouped in the centre, as seen here, but for the Mark II models the speedometer and rev counter were re-sited in front of the driver. Picnic tables and rear-seat heating were provided (RIGHT).

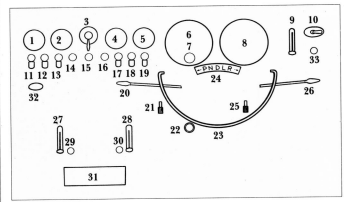

1	Ammeter	17	Map light switch
2	Fuel gauge	18	Electric screen wiper control
3	Exterior lights switch	19	Electric screen washer control
4	Oil pressure gauge	20	Automatic transmission lever
5	Water temperature gauge	21	Clock setting
6	Revolution counter	22	Headlamp dip switch
7	Electric clock	23	Horn ring
8	Speedometer	24	Automatic transmission and flasher warning
9	Choke (2.4 model only)	25	Trip recorder setting
10	Intermediate gear hold (automatic model only)	26	Direction indicator and flasher lever
11	Interior lights	27	Heater control (temperature)
12	Panel light	28	Heater control (volume)
13	Heater fan control	29 and 30	radio controls
14	Ignition switch	31	Radio panel
15	Cigar lighter	32	Scuttle vent lever
16	Starter button	33	Brake fluid level indicator

power without risk of wheelspin or axle tramp, which had afflicted the earlier 3.4's under heavy use of the right foot from rest.

The 3.8 was a natural for racing and it continued Jaguar's domination both in Great Britain and mainland Europe. Roy Salvadori enjoyed considerable success and in May 1960 he headed Stirling Moss and Graham Hill home in similar cars. Jack Sears, no newcomer to this form of racing, started driving Jaguars regularly with distinction. The late Colin Chapman, founder of Lotus Cars, took one victory during the year in a Coombs car before ordering one for personal use on the road. In 1961 Bruce McLaren and John Surtees joined in the fun, though Salvadori, Hill and a very fast young man called Mike Parkes were the most successful that year. In Germany Peter Lindner won a six-hour race and a twelve-hour race at the Nürburgring, and in France Bernard Consten clocked up the first of his four successive wins in the prestigious Tour de France.

The sensation of the 1961 Motor Show was the Mark X, which replaced the Mark IX. It was an entirely new car and employed, for the first time on the range of large cars, unitary chassis-less construction. Its entirely new shape, with great bulbous sides which now look somewhat dated, was designed for the American market. By US standards, it was not particularly large. By European standards, it was massive!

■ There were changes to the dash layout on the Mark II, although the traditional walnut veneers and leather were retained. These very fast small saloons made very good police cars and many British police forces ran fleets of them.

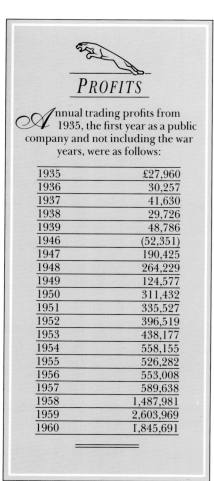

PROFITS

nnual trading profits from 1935, the first year as a public company and not including the war years, were as follows:

1935	£27,960
1936	30,257
1937	41,630
1938	29,726
1939	48,786
1946	(52,351)
1947	190,425
1948	264,229
1949	124,577
1950	311,432
1951	335,527
1952	396,519
1953	438,177
1954	558,155
1955	526,282
1956	553,008
1957	589,638
1958	1,487,981
1959	2,603,969
1960	1,845,691

■ *The Mark II's were an ideal businessman's express. They were stylish, fast, reliable and, like all Jaguars, exceptional value for money. To the Jaguar company they brought increased production and financial stability, aiding the expansion that seemed to be unstoppable in the 1950s.*

Powered by the three-carburettor version of the 3.8 engine as seen in the last of the XK 150's and the E-type, which had been announced a few months before, the Mark X was a respectable performer in spite of its vast weight (it tipped the scales at 35 cwt). The most significant mechanical development was the new independent rear suspension, first seen on the 'E' and included in every new Jaguar until the 1986 XJ40.

This rear suspension unit, consisting of transverse tubular lower links and universally-jointed halfshafts, plus four combined coil-spring and telescopic shock absorber units, was housed in a separate steel shell, or sub-frame, which was rubber-mounted to the body. It was further located by radial arms. Though heavy, it gave excellent roadholding and a superb ride, having been developed by Bob Knight.

Many orders were placed for the Mark X and praise was showered on it by all and sundry. The model looked to be a great success and in many ways it was, though, having been announced a bit too soon, it had a number of problems which took time to eliminate. What mattered was that it was the beginning of a concept which, with gradual improvements, would take Jaguar to its pinnacle of automotive merit. The brilliant Jaguars of the seventies and eighties are the offspring of the Mark X of 1961.

The Mark II's continued to dominate the race tracks in the early sixties. Both Parkes and Sears took victories in 1962, though it was Graham Hill who was by far the most successful that year. However, the large American saloons began to infiltrate Jaguar territory. Dan Gurney had brought over a massive Chevrolet Impala in 1961 and only the loss of a wheel had prevented his almost certain victory. A pair of Chevy II's campaigned

The smooth and slick new Jaguar Mark Ten.

...*and here is high speed luxury*

WITH the Jaguar Mark Ten, announced today, Sir William Lyons must have given his designers a free hand because in every major component and every small detail it achieves a new high level of splendid travel.

From the convenience of spring-assisted doors to high-speed travel touching 120 m.p.h. in complete luxury, the Jaguar Mark Ten bears the stamp of quality all the way—including disc brakes on all four wheels.

"Mail" Motoring Correspondent

outstanding flexibility which made travel in traffic easy.

At every opportunity for overtaking the car glided away, the steering positive with its power assistance, the visibility excellent and the comfort superb.

that the body is insulated from all noise and vibration.

Discs all round

The combination of disc brakes at the front and drum at the rear may be acceptable in some circum-

♦JAGUAR♦
MARK X SALOON

BODY STYLE(s): Large Saloon
ENGINE: XK Twin overhead cam
  6 cyl, 3781 cc
MAX POWER: 265 bhp
TIME: 0–60 10.8 secs
MAX SPEED: 120 mph
QUANTITY MADE: 13,382
PRICE: £2392
ANNOUNCEMENT DATE: Oct 1961
IN PRODUCTION: 1961–1964

■ *The massive Mark X caused a sensation at the 1961 London Motor Show and the motoring journalists, not for the first time with a Jaguar model, vied with each other to project the aura of this new flagship.*

regularly during the 1962 season and, although the Jaguar remained on top for most of the year, by the end its supremacy was toppled. An American, Kelsy, made a very good start at the May Brands Hatch meeting and as Kelsy had a great deal more power, there was no way that Salvadori could find a way past.

The year 1963 started well, with victories for Hill and Salvadori, but then Jack Sears appeared on the scene with a well-sorted and enormously powerful Ford Galaxie. He was unbeatable and he ended Jaguar's decade of supremacy. There were odd exceptions. Sears' Galaxie was missing from the Motor six-hour event, and though several other Galaxies were entered,

Jaguars finished first and second. The result would have been 1-2-3 for Jaguar, had not the leading 3.8 been disqualified for a minor infringement. The European Touring Car Championship was founded in 1963. Peter Nocker, driving Peter Lindner's Mark II, won it and the small Jaguar saloons took club drivers all over the world to a large number of wins.

An additional model, the S-type, was introduced in 1963. It was a most pleasing compromise, both aesthetically and mechanically, being based on the Mark II but benefiting from the new independent rear suspension. The styling was a little revised at the front and the roof line was flatter, providing greater headroom in the back. The rear was obviously inspired by the Mark

■ The Mark X saloon, which replaced the Mark IX in 1961, was different from its predecessor in many ways. The design and specification were modernized and the car no longer had a traditional chassis. It retained the faithful XK engine, in 3.8-litre form, but the body was larger than ever (the car was clearly aimed at the American market). Unfortunately, the model suffered from a number of small problems and, although some large export orders were taken, it was never as successful as hoped.

EMPIRE-BUILDING

In the early 1960s Sir William Lyons followed a pattern of acquisitions that is all too familiar these days. Diversification enabled Lyons to build up an engineering empire (sadly, it was not to last, as most of the once-famous names were to disappear under British Leyland rationalization). Guy Motors, founded in 1914, had been notable for introducing four-wheel brakes, Great Britain's first six-wheeled double-decker bus and the world's first six-wheeled double-decker electric trolley bus. During World War II the Ant, Quad-Ant and Lizard military vehicles were developed, as was the first British rear-engined, four-wheel-drive armoured car. An important innovation on the armoured car was its 'welded' Bullet-Proof Homogeneous Unmachinable Plate! This meant that riveted steel panels were no longer needed and the new plate gave superior protection at lower cost (Great Britain saved £100m on tank production by this method). It also enabled the car to wade.

By the early sixties Guy Motors had financial troubles and Lyons acquired the assets from the Receiver. The once-proud name was restored and the manufacture of lorries and passenger vehicle chassis flourished. In 1967 a new range was developed, appropriately named the 'Big J' models.

The Coventry Climax company began in 1903 by concentrating on producing engines. They were fitted in cars, boats, aeroplanes, and even the snow tractors used by Sir Ernest Shackleton's 1914 Imperial Trans-Antarctic Expedition. After 1945 the firm pioneered the fork-lift truck in Great Britain. Wally Hassan joined Coventry Climax from Jaguar and in 1950 the government asked the company, which had made fire-pumps during the war, to develop a new range that would be twice as powerful, yet half the weight! This challenge was met and the stimulus provided an engine that was used to good effect in motor racing by such illustrious names as Cooper and

Lotus. Success in the lower echelons of the sport led to the building of a Formula One engine. The 2½-litre power unit took Jack Brabham, driving a Cooper, to his world championships in 1959 and 1960. Jim Clark repeated the feat with the 1½-litre Climax-powered Lotus in 1963 and 1965. Jaguar acquired Coventry Climax in 1963 and with it that distinguished engineer, Walter Hassan. The company remained successful under Jaguar control, but the same cannot be said of its fate thereafter. In 1964 Lyons completed his acquisitions with the purchase of Henry Meadows Ltd. which, since its founding in 1919, had carried out a wide range of engineering work, including the manufacture of engines for Lagonda, Invicta, Frazer Nash, Lea Francis and H.R.G. The firm later turned to engines and transmissions for marine applications which, together with general engineering work and assembly of engines and transmission units for Guy, continued under the Jaguar umbrella until Meadows was closed down by BL in the seventies.

■ The Mark II saloons dominated saloon car racing all over Europe, clocking up a prodigious number of victories, and their dominance was strengthened by the addition of the 3.8 version. They also set speed and endurance records and for several years dominated the Tour de France. Even the superior roadholding of the nimble Jaguars could not, however, match the American giants, with their massive V8 engines, which appeared on the British circuits in the early 1960s.

X and the boot capacity was increased by 7 cubic feet.

The 3.4 and 3.8-litre engines were offered. Though they cost only a couple of hundred pounds more, the S-types had considerably improved ride and roadholding over the Mark II's and more modern styling but they did not seem to catch on. They sold well by others' standards but not by Jaguar's. Furthermore, the range was becoming rather too large and fragmented. Some modernization and rationalization were urgently needed.

■ The S-type, which joined the range in 1963, was a happy compromise between the Mark II models and the Mark X. Apart from a little re-styling, it benefited from a larger boot and the new independent rear suspension as fitted to the Mark X.

♦ J A G U A R ♦
S - T Y P E S A L O O N

BODY STYLE(s): Medium Sized Saloon
ENGINE: XK Twin overhead cam
  6 cyl, 3442 & 3781 cc
MAX POWER: 210 bhp & 220 bhp
TIME: 0–60 13.9 secs & 10.2 secs
MAX SPEED: Not Available & 121.1 mph
QUANTITY MADE: 9830 & 15,070
PRICE: £1669 & £1758
ANNOUNCEMENT DATE: Sept 1963
IN PRODUCTION: 1964–1968

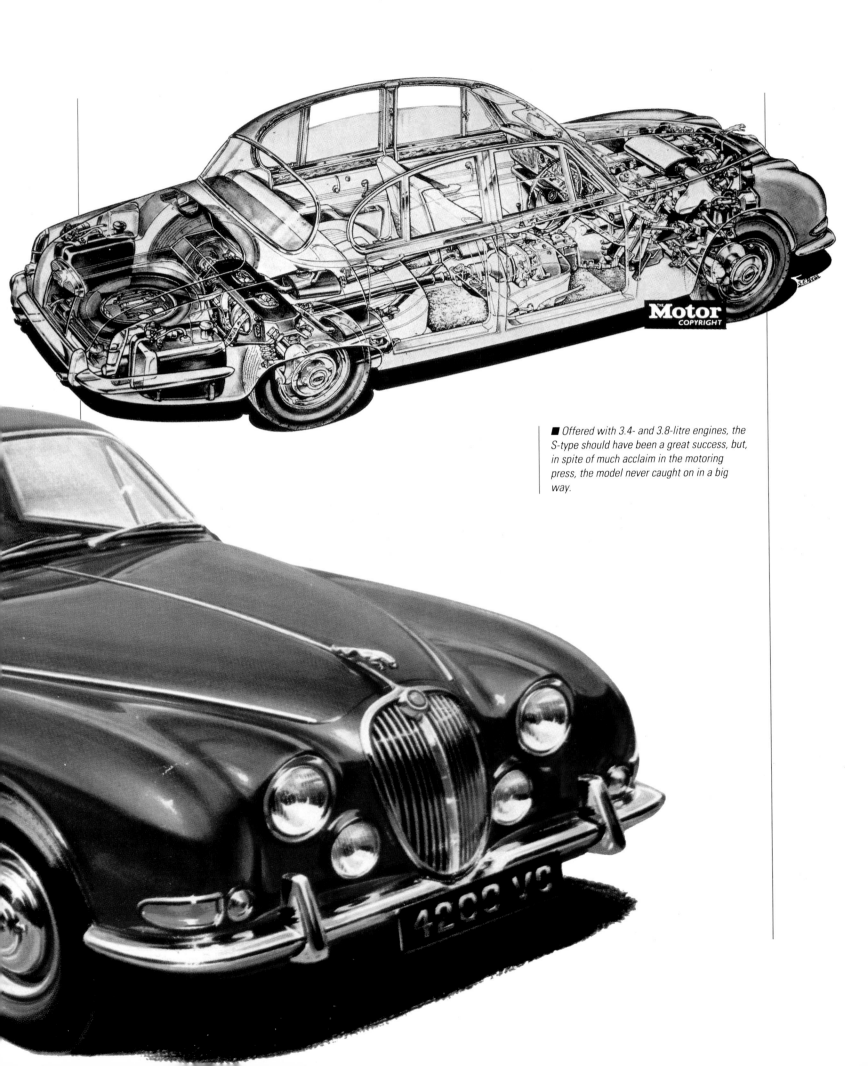

■ Offered with 3.4- and 3.8-litre engines, the S-type should have been a great success, but, in spite of much acclaim in the motoring press, the model never caught on in a big way.

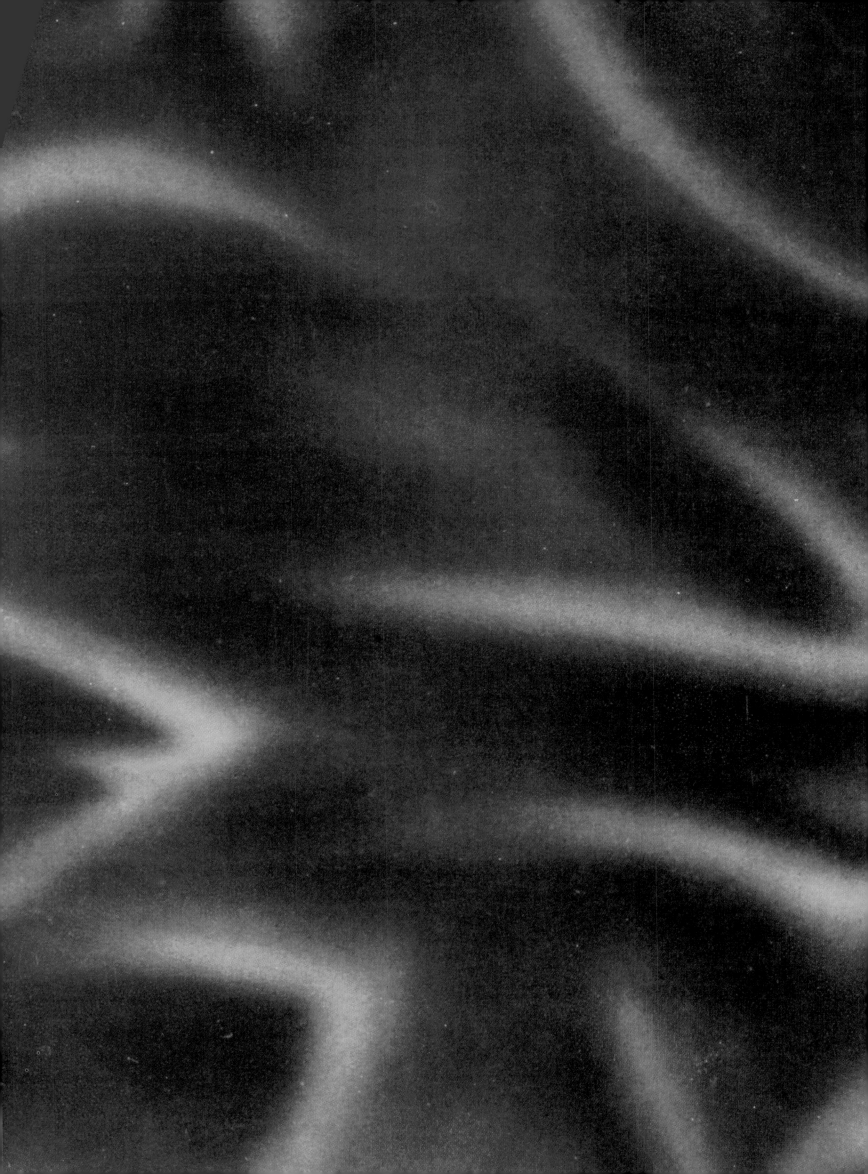

CHAPTER FIVE

THE RACING CATS

The D-type was to win at Le Mans three times and become, to many, the epitome of the post-war sports racing car.

There is no doubt that one of the most important factors in the Jaguar success story was the publicity generated and the image gained by their outstanding achievements in motor sport, especially racing. Lyons was shrewd enough to see the enormous potential of success on the famous race tracks of the world. Le Mans, more than any other event, attracted worldwide publicity and in those days motor racing was a relatively inexpensive form of advertising. With the designing of the brilliant XK engine and Lyons' genius for styling, Jaguar had the products. But it was motor racing that put the company on the world map.

Following the exploratory entry of three relatively standard XK120's in the 1950 Le Mans race and their surprisingly good showing, Heynes and England realized that a specially-built car would stand a good chance of success. The XK made a brilliant road car, but it was not designed for racing. Most of the basic elements, however, would, if modified, lend themselves to competition. The chassis was too heavy, and stronger than necessary, but the engine would be ideal if a little more power could be extracted from it. The front suspension already fitted the bill, but the body was too heavy and had not been designed with aerodynamics in mind.

So a pattern developed in the engineers' minds. If they could use the magnificent engine, with a little tuning, in a lighter chassis with a similar suspension and clothe all this in a lightweight, aerodynamically-designed shell, such a machine would stand a very fair chance against the might of the most famous racing names. Thus was the C-type born. It was known at the factory as the XK120C, with the 'C' standing for 'competition'. The late Harold Hastings of *The Motor* once claimed to me that he had been the first to coin the name 'C-type'. Certainly it stuck.

Lyons had decided at the 1950 Le Mans event to build a sports racing car for the following year's race. Heynes carried out the basic design of the C-type and Bob Knight was given responsibility for developing the project. Malcolm Sayer drew a most handsome, and above all efficient, shape for the body which was rather reminiscent of the pre-war T57 'Tank' Bugattis. This body enclosed a fully triangulated space-frame chassis made from differing sizes of round tubing and sheet steel bulkheads, welded to the frame fore and aft of the cockpit, considerably stiffening the structure.

Whereas the front suspension followed XK practice quite closely, with wishbones, telescopic shock absorbers and springing by torsion bars, the rear set-up was very different. A single transverse torsion bar was employed with the Salisbury axle, which was located by a pair of radial arms. An 'A' bracket gave lateral location and was designed to reduce the right rear wheel's penchant for lifting and therefore spinning by a torque effect. Braking was provided by a new Lockheed two-leading shoe, self-adjusting arrangement. The 120's recirculating-ball steering was replaced, to good effect, by rack and pinion. For the C-types, the exhaust valves of the XK engines were enlarged from 1$\frac{7}{16}$ in to 1$\frac{5}{8}$ in, the exhaust porting from 1$\frac{1}{4}$ in to 1$\frac{3}{8}$ in. By using a camshaft with $\frac{3}{8}$-in lift rather than $\frac{5}{16}$ in, the valve lift was increased and modifications to the valve springs allowed the engine to rev higher. The resulting power output was a little over 200 bhp.

Three C-types were finished just in time for the 1951 Le Mans 24-hour race. The competition consisted of six Lago Talbots, the 1950 winners, 2$\frac{1}{2}$-litre and 4-litre Ferraris, three 5.4-litre Chrysler-engined Cunninghams, five Aston Martins, and a 3.8-litre Nash-engined Healey.

♦ JAGUAR XK120C ♦
C – T Y P E

BODY STYLE(S): Sports Racing Car
ENGINE: XK Twin overhead cam 6 cyl, 3442 cc
MAX POWER: 200 bhp
TIME: 0–60 8.1 secs
MAX SPEED: 143.7 mph
QUANTITY MADE: Works Cars 11 Production Cars 43
PRICE: £2327
ANNOUNCEMENT DATE: Works Cars June 1951 Production Cars July 1952
IN PRODUCTION: Works Cars 1951-1953 Production Cars 1952–1953

■ The XK120C, or C-type as it became widely known, was the company's first purpose-designed sports racing car. It was designed with one object in mind, to win at Le Mans and gain for Jaguar the worldwide publicity that would follow success in the French 24-hour classic. After three privately-entered XK120s had, to everyone's amazement, threatened success in 1950, Lyons gave Heynes the go ahead to design a car to win the event. He was not slow to take up the challenge: the sketch (right) from the Jaguar archives, shows early thoughts on the distribution of the principal weight masses.

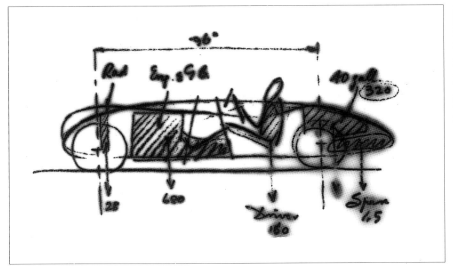

F.R.W. 'LOFTY' ENGLAND

*L*ofty England, who became Jaguar's famous Competitions Manager, characteristically towers above everybody else in most of the photographs of the company's racing exploits.

Following an apprenticeship with Daimler, he became a racing mechanic and had a succession of jobs working for, or on the cars of, such illustrious names as Birkin, Lord Howe, Whitney Straight, ERA and Dick Seaman. After a spell with Alvis, he joined Jaguar as Service Manager after the war.

That was for many years his official role, but with his competition experience – he himself had raced – he was naturally involved in Jaguar's first tentative steps into the motor racing world. He added a shrewd tactical brain to his practical knowledge and masterminded the many Jaguar wins. As several drivers found to their cost, he was very much 'in charge' and would brook no disobedience.

He rose through the company and when Lyons finally stood down, though advancing in years himself, he was the natural successor. His short tenure at the top was a difficult one because it was during the British Leyland era. He soon retired and went to live abroad, though he continued his association with the company, acting in the eighties – and his seventies – as a roving international ambassador.

Rainy weather prevailed in practice and led to several incidents. The race began in similar conditions, but Stirling Moss, in spite of his tender years, was a master of wet conditions and within three laps he was in the lead. Although circulating well within his capabilities, he broke the lap record several times and set so cracking an early pace that the Gonzales/Marimon and Rosier/Fangio Talbots eventually had to retire with problems brought on by attempting to match it.

With a sixth of the race gone, the C-types were lying in the first three places and things were looking good for the Jaguar team. They took a dramatic turn for the worse, however, when the Biondetti/Johnson car retired with a broken oil pipe flange. There were immediate fears that this annoyingly minor complaint might afflict the remaining Jaguars and when the Moss/Fairman car retired with engine maladies brought on by the same problem, the Jaguar camp was pessimistic about the chances of its final car escaping. All was well, however, and the Walker and Whitehead car circled lap after lap like clockwork to take a very fine win. During the second half of the race, there was little competition and they reduced their pace in favour of reliability. At the finish they were more than 60 miles ahead of the nearest Talbot, in spite of conditions that had included a thunderstorm and fog.

Moss had shown that the Jaguars were the fastest cars in the race and probably the most aerodynamic and the best-prepared. It was a triumph not only for the Jaguar company at its first serious attempt and the C-type in its debut race, but also for Great Britain. Since the great days of the Bentleys, British cars had not distinguished themselves in international motor sport

and the victorious Jaguars contrasted sharply with the hopeless B.R.M. debacle of the same period. Later in the year, Moss gained some consolation for his retirement in France, when he gained his second successive win in the classic T.T., this time piloting a works C-type.

The 1952 Le Mans race was a disaster for Jaguar. After the Mille Miglia, Moss, having been impressed by the straight-line speed of the Mercedes-Benz, had stressed that his car needed more power, and a new, more streamlined body with a longer nose and tail was quickly constructed. This new, lower body necessitated revisions to the cooling system. Since they were hastily made at the last moment, there was insufficient time for proper testing. All three cars overheated damaging the engines, and went out of the race early on. The episode was all the more galling because, as it turned out, the previous year's cars would almost certainly have won, and when poor Pierre Levegh hit trouble in his Talbot after driving singlehandedly for 23 hours, the Mercedes inherited a victory it barely deserved.

■ In June, 1951, three brand new C-types were entered at Le Mans. Two of the cars retired, including the Moss/Fairman car (seen here with Stirling at the wheel), but Peter Walker and Peter Whitehead were victorious.

Apart from the works competition C-types, Jaguar built a limited number of 'production' C-types for sale. These were intended for aspiring club drivers and allowed them to compete, especially in the United States, with comparable Ferraris. The cars were very similar to the 'works' cars apart from a little trimming and a horn which allowed the C-type to be used on the road! A number of them campaigned with success in some of the furthest corners of the world, but the C-type was always more at home on the fast circuits (that is precisely what it was designed for) than on the smaller, tighter circuits used for more minor events. For this reason, and also because the factory never really bothered with less glamorous events than the Le Mans races, the C-type did not have an enormous list of successes.

The Le Mans race of 1953 hit an all-time high in terms of prestige. A record number of 18 manufacturers was officially represented and most of the top Grand Prix drivers of the era competed, including three world champions, Farina, Ascari and Fangio. A new Manufacturers' Championship accounted for the extra interest and of the famous names only Mercedes, preparing to return in 1954, was missing.

Connoisseurs expected to see Alfa Romeo and Ferrari duelling for top honours, especially with the Jaguars outwardly unchanged from their 1951 appearance. However, these C-types were significantly changed below the skin. First and foremost, their new disc brakes, first tried on the Mille Miglia and then further developed, were to play no little part in the proceedings. Three twin-choke Weber carburettors, a lightened body and chassis, a

■ *The year 1952 was a disaster for Jaguar, with all three of its cars retiring early. But 1953 proved to be a glorious triumph for the Coventry marque. Ranged against many of the world's greatest names, Duncan Hamilton and Tony Rolt (the latter photographed below bathing his eyes and showing the gruelling strain of the endurance classic) drove an inspired race to win; and their team mates came second and fourth.*

FAUX PAS AT LE MANS!

One of the dedicated Jaguar racing mechanics was a chap called Joe Sutton, who joined Jaguar in 1946. Now in his eighties, he has many stories from the 'good old days'.

'One year at Le Mans, Lofty decided that he didn't want too many people milling round the pits and getting in the way, so he had some badges made and nobody without a badge was allowed in.

'One of our younger lads, Gordon Gardner, was on the door to the pits when this fellow, without a badge, walks up and says he would like to see Lofty. "I should bugger off if I was you, mate," said Gordon in his usual blunt way. "He's busy at the moment."

'It was Prince Bernhardt of the Netherlands!

'Luckily Lofty explained and smoothed things over and he took it very well.'

■ *FAR RIGHT* For a comparatively small outlay, Jaguar achieved worldwide fame as a result of its racing success, which was astutely exploited by the company's advertising men.

■ The secret of Jaguar's success at Le Mans was their new disc brakes. Developed jointly by Jaguar and Dunlop, they were much more efficient than the drum brakes used hitherto. The new brakes allowed the C-types to set a scorching pace until the opposition gradually fell by the wayside.

revised, stronger rear suspension, and a triple-plate Borg and Beck clutch, plus many minor changes, completed the evolution.

Just four laps into the race, Moss, this time paired with Peter Walker, took the lead from the 4½-litre Ferrari that Villoresi was sharing with Great Britain's Mike Hawthorn. Moss, as usual, set a pace which stretched the opposition, but within an hour his famous bad luck afflicted him yet again and he was forced into the pits. Fuel starvation was the problem and another stop was necessary before the blockages were eliminated. These stops relegated him to 21st position.

Meanwhile Rolt, who had been sitting patiently in third place, speeded up and took the lead. He and Hamilton then maintained a pace that caused their rivals, in trying to match the pace, to fall by the wayside with a host of problems. The C-type's disc brakes contributed greatly to the fast lapping, allowing the drivers to brake far later than other drivers and to brake again and again from high speed with regularity and security. The mists often experienced early on the Sunday morning emphasized the quality of the disc brakes, since drivers with conventional drum brakes had to be much more cautious in judging their braking distances.

While the leading 'C' maintained its position – by nightfall, only one Ferrari and one Alfa on the same lap – the Whitehead/Stewart 'C' was circulating steadily two laps behind and Moss and Walker, having driven through the field, were on the same lap in seventh place. After 12 hours the Alfas were out and the only possible threat to the Jaguars was the Ferrari of Ascari and Villoresi, still in second place but now two laps down. A few hours later, the Ferrari's clutch gave up. Rolt and Hamilton took a superb, well-earned victory, setting the first 100+ mph average for the French classic and breaking the 4000-km barrier. Moss and Walker crossed the line in second place and Peter Whitehead and Jimmy Stewart, in fourth place, missed making it a Jaguar clean sweep by only 20 km.

■ *TOP LEFT* In 1953 Jaguar had the luxury of a spare car and the two number 18s caused no little confusion among the French officials, who fined Lyons for having both on the circuit!

■ *CENTRE LEFT* Jack Fairman stands on the pit counter behind Lofty England.

■ *BOTTOM LEFT* Ted Brookes (left) and two other mechanics line up behind the Belgian entry C-type of Laurent and de Tornaco, which finished ninth in 1953.

■ *ABOVE* Peter Walker leads two Cunninghams away at the start of the 1951 race, which 24 hours later he and Whitehead won.

■ TOP RIGHT *Victory after 24 hours in their disc-braked C-type was sweet for Hamilton and Rolt.*

■ CENTRE RIGHT *Peter Whitehead (left) and Ian Stewart finished in fourth place in 1953.*

■ BOTTOM RIGHT *Peter Walker was one of the finest British drivers of the early 1950s and, having shared victory with Peter Whitehead in 1951, he partnered Moss to second place in 1953.*

■ BOTTOM FAR RIGHT *Young Stirling Moss considerably enhanced his rapidly growing reputation with a victory in an XK120 in the Tourist Trophy. He joined the Jaguar works team soon after.*

'THE SUNDAY TIMES' ON 'THE GREAT BRITISH SPORTSCAR' OF 1953

'The importance of the dramatic British victory at Le Mans last weekend, when Jaguars took three of the first four places in the fiercely exacting twenty-four-hours' race, winning at an average speed of over 105 mph, goes far beyond the traditional purpose of 'improving the breed'. British sports cars, tough, swift products of British engineering skill and sportsmanship are opening up dollar markets on a scale unthought of five years ago. 'In this market sports cars constitute the thrusting vanguard of the British motor industry . . . Their effect is greater than their actual value, for everyone who buys or sees a British sports machine is at once a more likely customer for a staider British car.

'The man who built the team was William Lyons, who is only 52 . . . He is its captain and sole selector. To say he inspires it would introduce a note of mysticism foreign to its outlook. Nor does he drive it, for that is foreign to his own character. He directs it, but he directs it with a sustained and compelling intensity of purpose. His is an example of individual enterprise on a scale uncommon in these days of impersonal corporate undertakings. 'Physically trim, immaculate in dress, he has the aura of power but not its trappings. No entourage of secretaries and personal assistants trails his unceasing movement around the great modern factory the firm moved into 18 months ago, or to its growing outposts abroad – Lyons has made four trips to New York in the past three months. 'There is an American tang to his utter dedication to his concern. One feels he could appear at a Chamber of Commerce luncheon at Detroit, and be betrayed only by his accent, or perhaps his plain tie.'

First, second and fourth places against the might of the racing world was a splendid achievement. The publicity department and Jaguar's suppliers were not slow to inform the world, and the benefit to sales was immeasurable.

A development car that was built during 1953 was very similar to the E-type which was to appear some seven years later. This car, known retrospectively as the C/D, was a prototype of the legendary D-type, which was unveiled early in 1954.

The D-type was more sophisticated in construction than the C-type and aerodynamically more efficient and for many people it has become simply *the* classic sports racing car of all time. It has often been likened to an aircraft on four wheels. Applying techniques learned during aircraft work in the war, Heynes and his team, by now unrivalled in the British motor industry, designed a car of largely monocoque construction.

Attached at the front to the central monocoque tub was a tubular sub-frame which carried the engine and front suspension. The tub was constructed of magnesium alloy and consisted of double-skinned front and rear bulkheads and large, tube-like sills. The one-piece bonnet hinged forward like the C-type's and the rear bodywork was removable. The

■ *The legendary D-type succeeded the C-type in 1954. Many aficionados consider the 'D' to be the classic post-war sports racing car. Incorporating much that had been learnt from the C-types, the D-type embraced aircraft technology in its construction and aerodynamics, which were the work of Malcolm Sayer.*

♦ J A G U A R   X K 1 2 0 D ♦
D – T Y P E

BODY STYLE(s): Sports Racing Car
ENGINE: XK Twin overhead cam
  6 cyl, 3442 cc
MAX POWER: 250 bhp
TIME: 0–60 4.7 secs
MAX SPEED: 162 mph
QUANTITY MADE: 71 (including 5 destroyed
  in factory fire and several dismantled)
PRICE: £3878
ANNOUNCEMENT DATE: Works Cars
  June 1954 Production Cars Aug 1955
IN PRODUCTION: Works Cars 1954–1956
  Production Cars 1955–1956

suspension was similar to the C-type's, particularly at the front, where it again employed wide-based double wishbones and torsion bars. The rear axle was attached directly to the rear bulkhead by four trailing arms, with a transverse torsion bar providing springing and an 'A' bracket giving lateral location.

To reduce frontal area, the engine was mounted at an angle of 8 degrees and, for the first time, dry-sumped to reduce the height of the engine further. A new gearbox was designed and even more efficient disc brakes were adopted; new Dunlop light-alloy wheels replaced the C-type's wire wheels. Aircraft-type flexible bag tanks were positioned in the tail and the filler was accessed through the distinctive streamlined headrest, which later gained a fin for high-speed stability.

Modifications to the engine increased the power output to 250 bhp. Inlet valves were increased to $1\frac{7}{8}$ in, the camshafts altered slightly and the exhaust manifolding improved.

Three of these very beautiful D-types lined up for the 1954 Le Mans race and 'should' have won. The race was a most frustrating one for Jaguar as the D-types were delayed by traces of fine grey sand in the fuel. There was talk of sabotage!

MALCOLM SAYER

*M*alcolm Sayer joined Jaguar in the early fifties from a background in the aircraft industry. Aerodynamics was his speciality and he is remembered with great admiration and affection by many of his colleagues.

His first creation for his new company was the body design of the first pure competition Jaguar, the C-type, to which, making extensive use of wind tunnels, he successfully applied aerodynamic theory.

There is a well-known saying in motoring circles that 'if it looks right, it probably is right'. There can surely be no better example of that principle than the legendary D-type.

The body was the work of Sayer, who later adopted the famous fin for high-speed stability at Le Mans. Apart from the D-type, Sayer's most famous achievement must be the E-type, the only production Jaguar that Sir William did not design. Later he was working, just before his premature death, on ideas for a mid-engined production car. Happily, he left the world one monument from this period, the glorious and beautiful XJ13 racing car.

■ TOP LEFT *The D-type's debut was a frustrating one. After two of the team cars retired with problems. Rolt and Hamilton only just failed to repeat their success of the previous year. These three famous D-types had the registration numbers OKV 1, OKV 2 and OKV 3, by which they are known today.*

■ LEFT *Revenge was gained when the D-type took its first victory in the 12-hour race at Rheims. Peter Whitehead and Ken Wharton took first place and were followed home by Rolt and Hamilton.*

The Ferraris did not have disc brakes, but their 4.9-litre engines provided plenty of power and Gonzales led initially. They may even have had an embarrassment of power in the wet conditions, allowing Moss to take the lead in his customary fashion. However, he and the other drivers were forced to visit the pits with misfiring problems which, though eventually traced to blocked filters and solved, cost valuable time. Moss then lost all his brakes at the end of the Mulsanne Straight and, though a trip up the escape road avoided a serious accident, his and Walker's race was run. The 'D' driven by Ken Wharton and Peter Whitehead lost most of its gears some time later and was forced to retire.

Meanwhile the Rolt/Hamilton car, its fuel problems eradicated, was circling very rapidly and, despite the appalling conditions, closing in on the leading Ferrari. Then, a little after 10 o'clock in the morning, a Talbot edged Rolt off the road and into a sandbank, forcing him into the pits. With only a few hours to go, the Ferrari refused to start after a routine pit stop and seven minutes were lost while a horde of Italian mechanics, rather more than was allowed, worked in panic on the car. Eventually it stuttered into life, but by then the Jaguar was only a minute and a half in arrears. In the torrential conditions Duncan Hamilton, not easily alarmed, noted that he was getting wheelspin at 170 mph! When Hamilton took over for his final spell, the 'D' was three minutes and fourteen seconds behind. He reduced this to one minute and 26 seconds, but then the road began to dry out, enabling Gonzales to use the big Ferrari's power to good effect. The Ferrari took victory by just two miles after 24 hours of flat-out racing.

Jaguar gained some consolation a month later at the 12 hour event at Rheims. Moss set a pace that destroyed the Ferraris and, after he had retired, his team-mates took the first two positions.

For 1955 Jaguar developed the 'long nose' D-types, so named because the bonnets were lengthened by 7½ in to aid penetration of the air. The engines

■ LEFT Tony Rolt, seen here at Le Mans in 1954, began racing before the war while at Eton. After the war, during which he spent some time in the infamous Colditz prisoner-of-war castle, he joined Jaguar, first as a reserve driver and then, after he had beaten the regulars, as a fully-fledged member of the team.

■ ABOVE The year 1955 saw the introduction of the 'long nose' D-types and an epic duel took place at Le Mans between Mike Hawthorn, for the Jaguar team, and Juan Manuel Fangio, in a 300SLR Mercedes Benz. It was the year of the dreadful Mercedes Benz accident in which 85 spectators and one driver were killed. The Mercedes was withdrawn, leaving victory to Hawthorn and Ivor Bueb, though not a victory to celebrate.

■ LEFT Their superb heritage, incredible performance (even by today's standards) and fabulous good looks, ensure that the D-types are among the most sought-after collectors' cars in the world.

benefited from new 'wide-angle' heads, which had larger inlet and exhaust valves with an inclination increased to 40 degrees. Power output was increased to 275 bhp at 5,750 rpm.

Le Mans that year was clouded by the crash which killed Pierre Levegh and 80 spectators. For this race Mercedes were back with their 300 SLR cars, which were fitted with the controversial hydraulically-operated air brakes in an effort to match the disc brakes of the Jaguars.

For the first two hours, three cars circulated in close company, breaking the lap record on no fewer than 10 occasions. They were Fangio in the Mercedes, Castelotti in the Ferrari and Hawthorn, who had now joined the Coventry team, in a D-type. The Ferrari could not stand the pace and retired with the lap record standing to Hawthorn. Then occurred the dreadful accident and in the ensuing mêlée the Fangio/Moss 300 SLR built up a two-

■ *LEFT AND ABOVE D-types competed far and wide in a whole variety of events from Daytona to Silverstone, both in the hands of factory drivers and private entrants and either in ex-works cars or, more generally, in the 'production D-types' produced with privateers in mind. Like the C-type, the 'D' was designed for victory at Le Mans, and it was less successful on the slower circuits.*

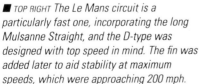
■ *TOP RIGHT The Le Mans circuit is a particularly fast one, incorporating the long Mulsanne Straight, and the D-type was designed with top speed in mind. The fin was added later to aid stability at maximum speeds, which were approaching 200 mph.*

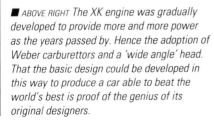
■ *ABOVE RIGHT The XK engine was gradually developed to provide more and more power as the years passed by. Hence the adoption of Weber carburettors and a 'wide angle' head. That the basic design could be developed in this way to produce a car able to beat the world's best is proof of the genius of its original designers.*

lap lead. Some hours later the whole Mercedes team was withdrawn on orders from Stuttgart and the lone 'D' of Mike Hawthorn and Ivor Bueb (the others having retired) went on to a hollow victory.

Jaguar returned to the famous track in 1957 but it looked initially as if it going to be as disastrous for the works team as the 1952 event. On the second lap Paul Frere, in one of the works D-types, overtook Jack Fairman, in another, as they came into the Esses; but, leaving his braking too late on the damp track, he hit the barriers and spun. Fairman managed to avoid him by spinning but was hit by de Portago, who was also having a 'moment'. The result was that two-thirds of the Jaguar team was out of the race with something like 23 hours and 55 minutes to go!

To make matters worse, the remaining Hawthorn/Bueb car had to pit a number of times with misfiring, which was eventually traced to a crack in a fuel line. By the time this was discovered, the car was down to 20th place and

■ TOP LEFT In 1957 the Belgians, Frere and Rouselle, finished fourth at Le Mans in their Ecurie Belge D-type.

■ LEFT AND ABOVE When Jaguar faltered at Le Mans in 1956 and the company retired from racing in the following year, the marque's mantle was taken up by the private team from Scotland, Ecurie Ecosse, which won twice.

Not surprisingly, a number of specialist racing car builders caught on to the effectiveness of the XK engine as a competition power-plant and units appeared in a diverse selection of machines.

These included cars built by Cooper, Tojeiro and HWM, but by far the most successful and numerous were the Lister-Jaguars. Built by the Cambridge-based engineering firm, George Lister & Sons, they were the creation of Brian Lister.

After fitting MG, Bristol and Maserati engines in his sports racing cars with mixed results, Lister tried an XK.

His driver was the fondly-remembered Archie Scott-Brown, who in spite of a deformed right arm was as quick as anybody in sports cars. In 1957 the duo took 11 wins out of 14 events and, as fame and news of these successes spread, a number of replicas was sold. Ecurie Ecosse was one customer. Another was Briggs Cunningham, whose Listers clocked up a number of successes in the United States with drivers such as Walt Hansgen.

In the following year the new models had bodies known today as 'knobbly' Listers and a brace of works cars was run with 3.8 XK engines. Scott-Brown tragically lost his life during the season. Others who piloted Listers that year were Hansgen, Stirling Moss and Ivor Bueb. Listers never distinguished themselves in the famous long-distance events, but they gained a prodigious number of wins in club and national events around the world before taking honourable retirement in late 1959.

although the pair drove valiantly and established the fastest lap, sixth position was their only reward. Ecurie Ecosse had made a single exploratory entry with one of their ex-works D-types and to their great joy, to say nothing of Jaguar's, it took a splendid victory.

Jaguar announced in October 1956 that it was retiring from racing, adding that it would be only a temporary sabbatical. Meanwhile the D-types, which, like the C-types before them, had been put into limited 'production', were raced widely by enthusiasts all over the globe, though, like the C-types, they were not suited to slow, tight tracks.

Today the Production D-types, let alone the ex-works cars, are among the most valuable and sought-after motor cars in the world, commanding quite ridiculous prices. The D-type was unquestionably brilliant on fast tracks. It was only really designed for Le Mans. And in 1957 those splendid privateers from Scotland, Ecurie Ecosse, made it a trio of wins for the 'D' and five in all in the 1950s for Jaguar.

ECURIE ECOSSE

*I*n less than 10 years, Ecurie Ecosse, the famed Scots team, graduated from three weekend drivers with a backstreet garage to a racing stable with international successes under its belt. It was formed and run by former driver, David Murray, and ace mechanic and tuning wizard, 'Wilkie' Wilkinson.

The team began in 1952 with three young drivers, Ian Stewart from Perthshire, Bill Dobson from Edinburgh and Sir James Scott-Douglas Bt. from Kelso, all of whom owned XK120's. Ten first places, six seconds and six thirds were gained from the first season, though these were mainly club events. Three C-types were acquired in 1953 and three continental events featured in that year's itinerary. Jaguar offered Ecurie Ecosse three disc-braked, ex-works C-types (which were being replaced by the new D-types) for the 1954 season. By then Dobson was no longer a member of the team and Ninian Sanderson and Jimmy Stewart, elder brother of the future world champion, Jackie, had joined.

Twelve wins from 17 starts in 1954 impressed Jaguar, who 'sold' the team three D-types in 1955. With these the Ecurie collected seven wins from a dozen events.

The years 1956 and 1957 really put the Scottish team on the international map. After a win at Spa and fourth at Rheims, Ecurie Ecosse entered a lone 'D' for the 24-hour Le Mans classic. It was their first attempt and Jaguar had cause to be extremely grateful to them. Two works cars were out in the first few minutes and the third was delayed with problems. The single car for Ninian Sanderson and Ron Flockhart had been only an exploratory entry, with a view to full-scale effort the following year. Luckily for Jaguar, the blue D-type with the white St. Andrew's Cross on its side took a most unexpected win. The following year the works team was missing, as Jaguar had by then retired. Jaguar honour and prestige were upheld, however, when Ecurie Ecosse, improving on their remarkable 1956 feat, took the first two places.

■ *ABOVE LEFT Norman Dewis and Ted Brookes, left, replace the spare wheel (obligatory at Le Mans) in its hinged compartment.*

■ *ABOVE From the racing D-type of the 1950s evolved the road-going E-type of the 1960s and 1970s; seen together, the lineage is obvious.*

■ *RIGHT Le Mans was a happy hunting ground with three victories in four years.*

■ *FAR RIGHT Three victories were not achieved without a great deal of testing and backroom work by the hardworking, loyal and highly capable Jaguar mechanics. Shown here is Norman Dewis, the chief tester, taking the first D-type round the banking at MIRA, the industry's testing ground.*

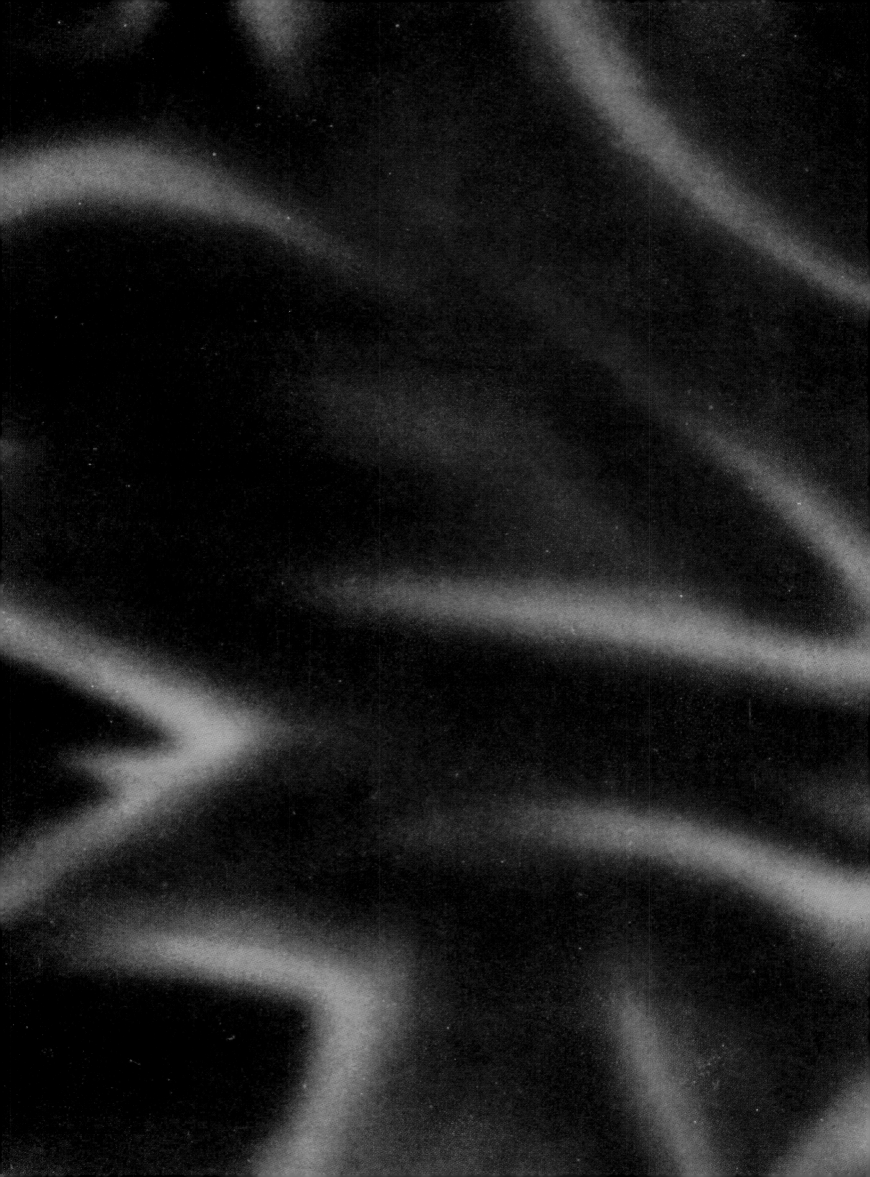

CHAPTER SIX

THE SENSATIONAL
XK-E

The E-type was introduced at Geneva in 1961; it would capture the world's imagination, and never let it go.

To many people the E-type is as sensational a car today as it was when it was launched in 1961. Then, of course, it was a sensation. It was vivacious, sensuous, shocking and fast – as much a symbol of the 'Swinging Sixties' as the Beatles or the mini-skirt. But a sign of its greatness was that it was no passing fad. Over the years the love affair between this beautiful sports car and enthusiasts everywhere has endured.

Enthusiasm is often kindled by rarity. The E-type is not rare and yet it is highly revered. If only a handful had been made, the car would be one of the most sought-after in the world. There are, it is true, faster cars today, though not too many in a straight line, and there are better-built, more sophisticated cars. But it is debatable whether there exists any more beautiful or downright exciting car today.

Nothing is perfect in the real world and the E-type was far from perfect. It was, however, a tremendous step forward. Just as the XK120 had brought racing car performance to the enthusiast in the street, so, 13 years later, did the E-type. And just as the XK120 put Jaguar way ahead of its rivals in the performance stakes, so the 'E' did the same.

The XK concept was, not surprisingly, aging by the late fifties. The engine was still a match for most and the 150's disc brakes were a great improvement; but the car was heavy, the chassis and live axle dated, and the body not to everybody's liking. The competition was catching up and in the United States cars were being fitted with vast V8's which gave superior acceleration. Sales were tailing off and Jaguar needed something sensational to survive in the sports car market. Bill Heynes' team had conquered the world at Le Mans, the pinnacle of international sports car racing; but it was urgent that their talents be turned to the bread-and-butter production cars. Thus Jaguar retired from racing, though it is not surprising that their thoughts for a road car should correspond closely to what they had been working on for the track.

♦ JAGUAR E-TYPE ♦
OPEN TWO SEATER

BODY STYLE(s): Roadster
ENGINE: XK Twin overhead cam
  6 cyl, 3781 cc
MAX POWER: 265 bhp
TIME: 0–60 7.1 secs
MAX SPEED: 149.1 mph
QUANTITY MADE: 942 (rhd)   6885 (lhd)
PRICE: £2098
ANNOUNCEMENT DATE: March 1961
IN PRODUCTION: 1961–1964

■ *The E-type took the D-type concept and adapted it for the road, making its level of performance available to the man in the street. Open and closed body styles were offered, both being strictly two-seaters. The interior was perhaps a little stark by Jaguar standards, but it was in keeping with the uncompromisingly sporting image of the 'E'.*

9600 HP

The E-type was bred from the racing cars and, in principle, had much in common with the D-type. Indeed, the prototype that was briefly seen before the emergence of the 'D', the 1953 car known as the 'C/D', bore a striking resemblance to the eventual E-type. The shape of the racing cars was determined by Jaguar's aerodynamicist, Malcolm Sayer. Indeed, much of the credit for their speed and stability is due to him. Using a wind tunnel to conduct tests, he applied aircraft principles to the D-type – the aircraft on wheels – and this was the E-type's heritage. The XKSS had been an attempt to modify the D-type for the road; the E-type was a 'D' designed for the road from the outset. (There were, in fact, thoughts of racing the car as well, but these were, sadly, not followed up until it was really too late.)

The shape was developed by Sayer and for once Sir William had little to do with the design of one of his production cars. He added his touch of genius in refining the detail work, but the actual shape was Sayer's. The mechanical design was carried out by Heynes, assisted by men such as Bob Knight, Tom Jones and Phil Weaver. The first prototype they built was rather smaller than the final car and was fitted with an aluminium 2.4-litre engine. The body was a monocoque like the D-type's and was constructed of aluminium, with a tubular sub-frame from the front bulkhead forwards carrying the engine, front suspension and steering. The rear suspension was a departure from D-type practice.

As the 'D' was designed for Le Mans, which is a high-speed circuit with few slow bends, a live axle was no disadvantage. The 'D' lost out, however, on slower, more twisty circuits. Heynes and Knight had therefore been experimenting with an independent rear suspension and had fitted a version of this to a new sports car which was known as 'E1A' (the 'A' standing for aluminium) and which was first running in May 1957.

The car was extremely light at 17 cwt and, despite its small engine, put up the impressive figures of a 0-60 time of 10.5 seconds and a top speed of 130 mph. A great deal of testing was carried out, after which a larger body was built. This was to be the final size and the car, known as the 'Pop Rivet

This E-type, now owned by the author, was a prototype car completed in mid-1960. The oldest E-type still in existence, it played a mixed but very busy part in the early days of the model. Having been used extensively for testing and development work in late 1960 and early 1961, it was lent just prior to launch to several eminent motoring journalists. The result was road tests and articles in such magazines as *Autocar, Autosport* and *Motor Racing*. With one or two lightening features, racing tyres and a 'breathed-on' engine, the car just achieved the magic 150 mph, though no standard E-type could quite duplicate the result.

For various reasons the factory had very few cars ready in time for the launch at the Geneva Motor Show in March 1961 and so Bob Berry drove 9600 HP to Geneva to be presented to the world's press. One or two last-minute hitches delayed his departure and it had to be a virtual flat-out run from Coventry to Geneva. He arrived with just 20 minutes to spare and the E-type, in more senses than one, had arrived!

Later, the car appeared in *Motor Sport* and *Motor*, among others, before being sold to former factory racing driver, Jack Fairman.

■ *ABOVE AND LEFT The simplicity of the E-type's clean lines was beautiful. Very early cars had external bonnet locks, as can be seen just behind the front wheel.*

♦ JAGUAR E-TYPE ♦
FIXED HEAD COUPE

BODY STYLE(s): Closed Two Seater
ENGINE: XK Twin overhead cam
   6 cyl, 3781 cc
MAX POWER: 265 bhp
TIME: 0–60 6.9 secs
MAX SPEED: 150.4 mph
QUANTITY MADE: 1798 (rhd)   5871 (lhd)
PRICE: £2197
ANNOUNCEMENT DATE: March 1961
IN PRODUCTION: 1961–1964

■ *Like the XK120 before it, the E-type brought racing car performance to the road and yet remained relatively sophisticated, with unprecedented levels of comfort for a sports car. The Fixed Head was the first E-type to be shown; it caused a sensation and a long queue was quickly formed to place orders.*

Special', was later made into a runner. A succession of prototypes was built and tested in the next few years until in 1961 the car, though barely ready, was announced.

The reaction from press and public alike was as sensational as the car. Jaguar was offering a 150-mph car with race-bred cornering and handling, unheard-of good looks, together with comfort, at an unbelievably low price. The orders flowed in. Very few cars were produced in the first year and the scarcity served to heighten the demand. It was an event to see an E-type and you certainly had to *be* someone to acquire one. The first customers, hand-picked by the Jaguar management, included many famous names. All this publicity enhanced the Jaguar name. If you could not afford a new E-type or needed more seats than it provided – or simply could not get one – you could drive a car made by the company that made E-types.

In spite of considering 3-litre and 3.4-litre engines, Jaguar launched the 'E' with the 3.8-unit fitted with three SU carburettors that had been developed for the 'S' version of the XK150. Helped by its more aerodynamic shape and lighter construction, the new car had a considerably higher top speed than the XK150. Acceleration was vivid but, thanks to the new rear suspension, the ride was excellent. For this level of performance the braking, even with discs all round, was barely adequate and the gearbox was considered slow; but these shortcomings were forgotten amid the outstanding qualities of what was a true 'classic' from the day it was launched.

Two body styles were offered. The Open version, known more often today as the Roadster, was a strict two-seater with a folding hood and

■ *The chassis of the XK's had gone and the construction, like that of the D-types, was monocoque. But, unlike the D-types, the 'E' had a new independent rear suspension.*

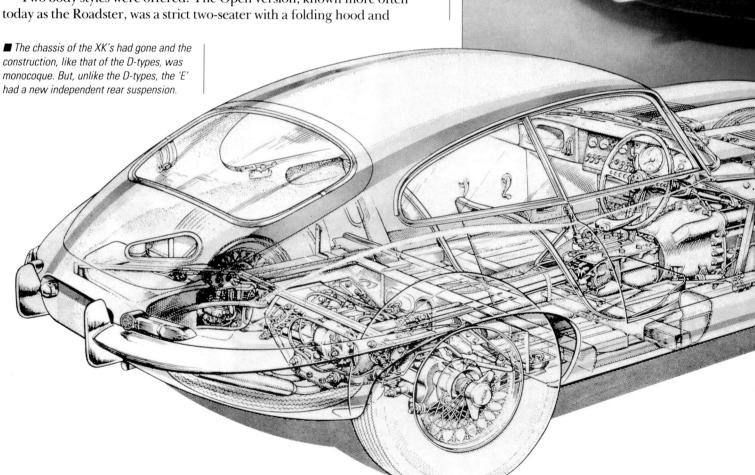

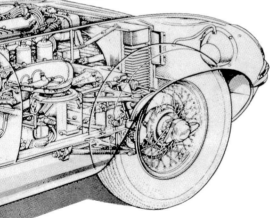

■ *ABOVE The independent rear suspension made an important contribution to the tremendous strides forward in ride and roadholding, which, allied to the XK unit in three-carburettor, 3.8-litre form, made the E-type a revelation on the road.*

E2A

*F*ollowing the building of the first, small prototype E-type, a second car was built with racing in mind and became known as E2A. This 'Competition E-type', as it was also known, was another step in the evolution from D-type to final E-type.

At one stage the intention was to field a team at Le Mans in 1958 or 1959; but it was not to be, and the single car built might never have seen action at all, but for the fact that Briggs Cunningham spotted it in the Experimental shop.

Cunningham was a racing enthusiast who had campaigned his own cars and D-types. He was also a Jaguar dealer in the United States. He managed to persuade Jaguar to lend him E2A to enter for the famous French race in 1960. After setting the fastest time in practice, the car failed to live up to its potential when the 3-litre engine (required by that time by the regulations) gave trouble and Walt Hansgen and Dan Gurney were forced to retire. These engines lacked development and the unit was replaced by a more normal 3.8 litre and used in the United States for several events. Hansgen took one win, but Jack Brabham was less lucky when he drove it.

optional hardtop. The Fixed Head had a fastback roofline and opening tailgate. It, too, was a strict two-seater, but it had more room for luggage. Opinion is divided as to which is the prettier, though perhaps rather more people favour the Open. The Fixed Head, however, has suffered the ravages of time rather better, owing to the added strength of the roof section, which lets in less water. At £1,830 for the Roadster and £1,954 for the Fixed Head, the E-types, in true Lyons style, were remarkable value for money.

Within a month or so of the new car's launch, Roadsters were supplied to two private racing teams which regularly campaigned Jaguar saloons in production-car racing, John Coombs and Equipe Endeavour. They were immediately taken to Oulton Park, where Roy Salvadori drove the Coombs car and Graham Hill the other. Ranged against them were the 250GT

■ *The XK engine produced 265 bhp in the E-type and the engine and front suspension were carried on a tubular front sub-frame, which attached to the monocoque at the front bulkhead. The radiator was carried on an additional frame at the front and on this was pivoted the forward-hinging bonnet, giving good accessibility to the engine and its auxiliaries.*

Ferraris of Whitehead and Jack Spears, plus Innes Ireland in an Aston Martin DB4GT. Salvadori led initially but suffered from fuel surge and braking difficulties. When he dropped back to third place, Graham Hill took up the challenge and, despite boiling brakes, gave the E-type a fine win first time out. In second place was a charging Ireland, closely followed by Salvadori, who a few weeks later led from flag to flag at Crystal Palace. Yet, in spite of these victories, brought about by some very fine driving, the E-type struggled to match the Ferraris, which were thinly disguised racers having the advantage of 300 bhp and weighing 6 cwt less. With factory assistance, the Coombs car was gradually developed, but meanwhile Ferrari was designing the legendary 250GTO to combat the E-type threat.

The 1962 production cars featured a number of small but significant improvements. Taller drivers found the E-type difficult, if not impossible, to get in and out of and to drive. To assist them, a footwell was added to the floor; and a dish was put in the rear bulkhead which allowed the driver's seat to be pushed further back. Whereas the large one-piece, forward-tilting bonnet had been locked down by a 'T' bar inserted externally, interior locks were now adopted. The louvres on the bonnet, formerly a separate pressing, were now an integral part of the bonnet top. (These subtle differences serve to distinguish the very early cars, which have become highly treasured collectors' items.)

In 1962 three E-types were entered privately for Le Mans. Victory was not a realistic aim, since the event was now dominated by pure racing machines, as the C-types and D-types had been. Indeed Jaguar had done much to foster the trend. Even so, the E-types did not disgrace themselves. Roy Salvadori and Briggs Cunningham, in the latter's Fixed Head, surprised everyone, including themselves, by finishing in fourth place.

Mainly, one suspects, with the big, heavy Mark X in mind, Jaguar decided that the E-type needed more torque than the 3.8 provided. By redesigning the block a cubic capacity of 4.2 litres was achieved. The enlarged engine had the same power output as the 3.8 but manifested a most useful increase in torque. As the engine was to be offered in the big saloon, it was natural also to fit it in the sports car.

The new cars, introduced in 1964, were virtually unchanged externally, apart from the addition of a '4.2' on the bootlid of the Roadster and the tailgate of the Fixed Head. Other improvements were made at the same time. An all-synchromesh gearbox was at last fitted – the earlier 'box, as well as being slow, had had no synchromesh on first and was definitely behind the times. The interior was outfitted with better seats and revised dashboards and a more effective servo improved the braking.

The early road tests of the 3.8 cars had been very promising, but the road cars were not truly representative of production cars and the 4.2 was thought by many to be a slower car. In fact, it was very similar in performance and with its improvements the 4.2-litre Series I, as these cars were later termed, is an excellent car.

Meanwhile the Coombs racing 'E' had been gradually lightened, first with a thinner-gauge steel body and then with a full aluminium-alloy monocoque. The remarkable XK engine was breathed upon and power output gradually increased. Graham Hill, world champion in 1962, carried out much of the testing, with the factory giving a fair degree of assistance. From this car the concept of the 'Lightweight E' developed. About a dozen of them were built

◆ JAGUAR E - TYPE ◆
4.2 FIXED HEAD COUPE
& OPEN TWO SEATER

BODY STYLE(s): Closed & Open Two Seater
ENGINE: XK Twin overhead cam
   6 cyl, 4235 cc
MAX POWER: 265 bhp
TIME: 0–60 7 secs (FHC)
MAX SPEED: 150 mph (FHC)
QUANTITY MADE: 9550 (Open)
   7770 (FHC)
PRICE: £1934 (Open)   £2033 (FHC)
ANNOUNCEMENT DATE: Oct 1964
IN PRODUCTION: 1964–1968

♦ J A G U A R ♦
E-TYPE 2+2

BODY STYLE(s): Closed Two/Four Seater
ENGINE: XK Twin overhead cam
   6 cyl, 4235 cc
MAX POWER: 265 bhp
TIME: 0–60 8.9 secs
   (automatic transmission)
MAX SPEED: 136.2 mph (automatic)
QUANTITY MADE: 5600
PRICE: £2245 (automatic £2402)
ANNOUNCEMENT DATE: March 1966
IN PRODUCTION: 1966–1968

■ *ABOVE To broaden the appeal
of the E-type for the family man, the 2 + 2
was introduced, but the modification did
nothing for the shape.*

■ *LEFT The XK engine was enlarged to 4.2
litres in 1964 and fitted to the E-type. The
main benefit was extra torque, not extra
speed, and one of the E-type's few
shortcomings was overcome when a new all-
synchromesh gearbox replaced the slow 'box.*

by Jaguar for private teams. They were built from the ground up with competition in mind and featured an aluminium tub, solidly mounted rear suspension, a very heavy but five-speed ZF gearbox, aluminium blocks for the engines, light-alloy wheels and improved braking. They enjoyed some success against the Ferraris, as when Hill beat Parkes in a GTO at the Easter Goodwood meeting, but generally the Lightweights were not successful. One probable explanation is that the factory never ran a works team nor ever threw themselves well and truly into developing and racing the 'E'.

That the E-types were strictly two-seaters naturally narrowed the market, because the man who wanted both to enjoy E-type motoring and have a young family was left with a choice of priorities. An additional model, introduced in 1966, made his life easier. Jaguar offered a '2+2' version of the E-type, with provision for two offspring, or at a pinch an adult or two, in the rear.

This new model was eight inches longer and two cwt heavier. The roof line was two inches higher and the windscreen looked, in comparison, very upright. The 2+2 was also distinguishable by the addition of a chrome trim below the side windows. With its extra weight and greater frontal area, the new model was not so quick as its sisters, but the extra size had the advantage of allowing Jaguar to offer automatic transmission for the first time on an E-type. This option widened the market and exports rose constantly.

In late 1968 the Series I was replaced by the Series II. Sadly, the beautiful shape was not improved. Engineering progress and contemporary safety regulations led to changes which did little to improve the car's looks. Most noticeable was the deletion of the headlamp covers and the headlamps themselves were set back and raised to achieve the statutory minimum height. Larger side and flasher lights appeared and the bonnet mouth was enlarged for the optional air-conditioning unit. Wrap-around bumpers, front and rear, contributed to the heavier look. At the rear, the bumpers were raised and below them sat much enlarged lamps and a square number

LIGHTWEIGHTS AT
LE MANS

For the 1963 Le Mans race Briggs Cunningham entered three Lightweight E's, but a mixture of misfortunes marred the event for the great American sportsman. The cars were numbered 14, 15 and 16, which corresponded with their registration numbers 5114 WK, 5115 WK and 5116 WK. The Lightweights were fitted with a ZF gearbox, which had the advantage of five gears; but '14' retired in the first hour with gearbox problems.

Nearly 4½ hours into the race, Bruce McLaren had the misfortune to experience a blown engine at around 180 mph in his Aston Martin, depositing a large amount of oil on the track. Number 15 slipped through, but Roy Salvadori in '16' had no chance and spun off, catching fire. He was not badly hurt, but the car was well and truly out. At quarter distance '15' was lying 16th, and by 10.30 next morning this had improved to seventh when the driver, Grossman, found he had no brakes approaching the corner at the end of the Mulsanne Straight at 165 mph! With the aid of some straw bales, he managed to stop the car, but the front end was by now very secondhand. He eventually managed to coax the car back to the pits where, with parts from '14', the car was repaired sufficiently for it to complete the race, which it finished in ninth position.

■ To improve the company's racing performance, Jaguar developed what has become known as the 'Lightweight E', about 12 of which were produced with aluminium monocoques and engine blocks.

♦ JAGUAR SERIES II ♦
E-TYPE OPEN,
FIXED HEAD COUPE
& 2 + 2

BODY STYLE(s): Roadster, Closed Two
Seater & Closed Two/Four Seater
ENGINE: XK Twin overhead cam
6 cyl, 4235 cc
MAX POWER: 177 bhp (net)
TIME: Not Available
MAX SPEED: 135 mph
QUANTITY MADE: 8630 (Open) 4860 (FHC)
5330 (2+2)
PRICE: £2117 (Open) £2225 (FHC)
£2458 (2+2)
ANNOUNCEMENT DATE: Oct 1968
IN PRODUCTION: 1968–1970

♦ THE 'LIGHTWEIGHT Es' ♦

CH. NO.	ORIGINAL OWNER	DRIVEN BY
850006	John Coombs	Roy Salvadori, Graham Hill, Jack Sears, Jackie Stewart & Brian Redman
850659	Briggs Cunningham	Walt Hansgen, Bruce McLaren, Augie Pabst
850660	Kjell Qvale	Ed Leslie & Frank Morrill
850661	Tommy Atkins	Roy Salvadori
850662	Peter Lindner	Peter Lindner & Peter Nocker
850663	Peters, Lumsden & Sargent	Owners
850664	Briggs Cunningham	Grossman & Cunningham
850665	Briggs Cunningham	Richards & Salvadori
850666	Peter Sutcliffe	Owner
850667	Bob Jane	Never known to race
850668	Dick Wilkins	Never known to race
850669	Phil Scragg	Hillclimbed by owner

■ *In spite of being driven by a number of top drivers, including Graham Hill (shown here), the Lightweight came too late and could not hope to compete against the Ferraris, which had been designed with racing solely in mind.*

■ *ABOVE The American sportsman and Jaguar distributor Briggs Cunningham had entered a team of three Lightweight E's at Le Mans in 1963 (see page 156). One of those cars returned to Le Mans in 1987, with its proud owner, Nigel Dawes. Not surprisingly, such cars have become prized collector's items.*

plate. The interior sprouted rocker switches and recessed door handles as demanded by the new regulations. All three models were produced in Series II form, but the 2+2 had one marked difference from its predecessor. To soften the severity of the windscreen rake caused by the higher roofline, the base of the screen was moved forward to just behind the bonnet line, increasing the rake by 7 degrees.

Mechanically there were some significant improvements, the most important of which was in braking. New Girling calipers, three-piston at the front and two-piston at the rear, meant that for the first time the E-type had really good brakes. Power steering was an optional extra – the E-type was moving away from its sporting pedigree and becoming more of a touring car. The performance suffered from the additional weight and aerodynamic impedimenta and cars exported to the United States were fitted with Stromberg carburettors to satisfy emission regulations, a change which also adversely affected performance.

For some time Bill Heynes had been toying with the idea of a V12 engine with a view to reviving Jaguar's dominance of sports-car racing. For the reasons already outlined, Jaguar had pulled out of the sport. Ideally Jaguar wanted to design a new engine that could be used in both a racing car and the

■ *ABOVE* The 2 + 2 was fairly popular in the United States, to which the vast majority of E-types were exported. The E-type was always known there as the XK-E, and sales benefited from the fame and image of the earlier XK's.

■ *LEFT* Its longer wheelbase enabled the 2 + 2 to carry two children and a certain amount of luggage. The extra length also allowed automatic transmission to be offered for the first time on an E-type.

■ LEFT Towards the end of 1967 revisions
were made to the appearance of the E-type
that were to culminate in the Series II model
introduced in October, 1968. These changes
were dictated by American regulations
regarding the height of lights, impact
resistance and exhaust emission. The interim
model shown here has become known as the
Series 1½. It differed from the later Series II
in various ways. The later car had
considerably revised rear lights and the front
sidelights became larger and moved below
the raised bumper blades.

■ ABOVE All three models came in for the
same treatment, including the 2 + 2, shown
here in Series 1½ form.

production range. The V12 found favour for a variety of reasons, the most
important being that it was still a comparative rarity, to be found in Italian
exotica such as Lamborghinis and Ferraris. A V8 was considered, but in
addition to technical arguments against it, there was the fact that it was
common in the United States, which since the war had been Jaguar's most
important market. To be different, something other than a V8 was required.
It all pointed to a V12. The maximum engine size for prototype sports-car
racing at that time was 5 litres and so this was the obvious starting point.

In 1963 Jaguar had taken over Coventry Climax, who made forklift
trucks but were world-famous for producing winning Formula One world
championship engines. Wally Hassan, who had left Jaguar in the early fifties
to join Climax, had designed these engines. With the acquisition of Climax,
Hassan was back in the Jaguar fold. Soon after, he brought in Harry Mundy,
with whom he had previously worked at Climax. Thus four brilliant
engineers were brought together to design the engine – Heynes, who
directed the project, Claude Baily, who had had a hand in the original XK,
Hassan and Mundy.

Heynes, always a great enthusiast for racing, built a single mid-engined prototype in the mid-sixties to which was fitted a twin-cam version of the V12 engine. This car was known as the XJ13 and was a pure evolution of the 'C', 'D' and 'E' shapes. The body was the work of Malcolm Sayer and was, as ever, a work of great art and efficiency. The construction was fully monocoque and employed the mid-mounted engine as a stressed member. To it were attached the ZF transaxle and rear suspension. The engine produced 502 bhp. Sadly, for a variety of reasons there was no great urgency in the project; it was not completed until 1966 and not tested until a year later, by which time it was already being superseded by an increasingly sophisticated form of racing engine.

Those who drove the car in testing were very impressed with it and, in spite of a dire lack of brakes, they put up very respectable lap times. David Hobbs set a record for the fastest lap around an enclosed circuit at MIRA, recording 161 mph in 1967. Unfortunately Norman Dewis, while lapping the same circuit for some filming, experienced a failure and both somersaulted and rolled. The extremely secondhand XJ13 was later rebuilt and is today the pride of Jaguar's growing collection.

■ The XJ13 one-off prototype sports racing car was the car with which Jaguar, had the company decided to come out of retirement in the mid-1960s, would have returned to the world's racing tracks to take on the might of Ferrari and Ford. As it was, the costs, after the company being away from the highly competitive sport for so long, and, above all, the difficulty of living up to earlier successes, told against a return and the magnificent XJ13, another Heynes and Sayer masterpiece, never saw competition.

EXPORTS

*I*n 1963 the American magazine, *Car and Driver*, voted the E-type the best all-rounder and at that time one-third of all Jaguars were going to that market. By the mid-sixties, Jaguar were shipping 500 - 600 cars a week to the United States, earning revenue of £7m per annum. The British Motor Corporation (BMC), with which Jaguar merged in 1966, was, by contrast, exporting at that time 20,000 cars a week with annual sales of £21m. According to a 1968 advert, Jaguar was selling 95 per cent of all E-types abroad through a network of 134 distributors and 960 dealers in 126 countries. At the New York Show that year, orders were taken for 2,500 E-types. There is no question that the E-type was one of the export success stories of all time, earning, as well as currency, that important intangible, prestige, for Great Britain around the world.

Meanwhile the decision had been taken to build the V12 for production in single-cam form – for reasons of underbonnet space, simplicity, cost and weight. The exciting new engine was destined for the new range of saloons to be announced, first with the familiar six-cylinder engine, in the late sixties. In order to prove the engine and give a boost to the flagging image of the E-type, it was fitted into the sports car and announced in 1971.

The V12E, as it has become known, or Series III, as is more correct, was considerably revised. The 2+2 wheelbase was adopted for the Roadster; and the Fixed Head, known as the 2+2, was available only in 2+2 form. Externally the car acquired a front grille in what had previously been an open mouth and the wheel arches grew small flares to accept the wider track and tyres.

Power steering coped with the extra weight and, as the car was longer, automatic transmission could now be accommodated on the Open model as well. The capacity for the production engines was 5,343 cc and power output was 272 bhp on four Zenith carburettors. The engine was to have used fuel

■ *ABOVE Like the original XK engine, the magnificent V12 was designed with saloon cars primarily in mind, but appeared first in a sports car. In 1971 the arrival of the Series III E-type was announced, with the V12 engine.*

■ *ABOVE RIGHT The V12 engine rejuvenated the performance of the E-type at a time when it was affected adversely by emission control regulations.*

■ *RIGHT The XK engine, shown here in later form with two Stromberg carburettors to satisfy emission regulations, could not match earlier output.*

■ *FAR RIGHT The V12 engine was a masterpiece from the Jaguar engineers and it received a rapturous welcome.*

injection and production was delayed when the manufacturer chosen to supply the injection equipment decided to abandon its manufacture. Braking was improved with vented front discs – just as well since, in comparison with the Series I this was, at nearly 29 cwt, a heavy car.

With the benefit of 5.3 litres, a manual Roadster could reach 60 mph in 6.4 seconds and had a top speed of 146 mph. In the American specification it took a second longer to 60 mph and, owing to emission control equipment, could only achieve 136 mph. By 1974, in fact, the 0-60 mph time had increased to eight seconds.

The V12 E-types were reasonably popular and slightly more than 15,000 were produced between 1971 and 1974, with 77 per cent being exported. The 2+2 was withdrawn in September 1973; the Roadster continued to be sold until February 1975. With the demise of the latter, Jaguar for the first time since 1948 listed no open sports car. This omission was an unfortunate sign of the times: every manufacturer believed that open cars would be outlawed in the major market, namely the United States.

Final sales and the Jaguar image were given a boost there when Bob Tullius of Group 44, based in Virginia, and Huffaker Engineering of California were commissioned to race specially prepared V12E's in the championships held on their respective coasts. They were particularly successful and Tullius became SCCS National Champion in 1975.

Thus the legendary E-type went out, just as it had come in, on a high note. Many people have questioned whether the 'E' should ever have been dropped. Many have asked whether it could be resuscitated. The truth is that the final cars took some selling, though in hindsight they have come to be better appreciated.

It is unlikely we shall ever again see a car so downright exciting and sexy as the E-type. The time was right for it and it has become quite simply the most famous sports car in the world. It fully deserved and deserves that epitaph.

■ *The V12 E-type was produced in only two body styles and the longer wheelbase of the 2 + 2 Fixed Head was adopted for the Roadster (shown here) as well. The new V12, though complex, was silky smooth, with good power output and torque, endowing the E-type once again with both performance and, most important for Jaguar, technical prestige.*

■ *RIGHT The 2 + 2 shape had never been a very happy one and, with its 'silent' engine and such refinements as power-steering, the Series V12 E-type was a very different car from the original 3.8's seen at the beginning of the Swinging Sixties.*

♦ **J A G U A R** ♦
SERIES III E-TYPE
OPEN TWO SEATER
& 2 + 2

BODY STYLE(s): Roadster & Closed Two/
    Four Seater Coupe
ENGINE: V12 5343 cc
MAX POWER: 272 bhp
TIME: 0–60 6.4 secs & 6.8 secs
MAX SPEED: 146 mph & 142 mph
QUANTITY MADE: 7990 & 7300
PRICE: £3139 & £3387
ANNOUNCEMENT DATE: March 1971
IN PRODUCTION: 1971–1975 1971–1973

■ *Flagging sales were given a filip in the United States when a couple of teams, including Group 44 (shown here), successfully raced V12 E-types before the E-type quietly bowed out. The Fixed Head ceased production in 1973, the Roadster two years later. It will be the early 1990s, if all goes according to plan, before Jaguar once again produces a genuine sports car to follow the XK's and E-types.*

THE LAST E-TYPES

*T*he last 50 V12 E-types to be produced were all painted black except one. The last but one was painted dark green for the Jaguar collector, Robert Danny. All 50 had a numbered plaque signed by Sir William Lyons and affixed to the dashboard.

Much sought after today, it seems incomprehensible that these last 50 should not have sold 'like hot cakes'.

But it was not so. The author remembers one example which sat in the showrooms of P. J. Evans, one of Lyons' original dealers, for several months awaiting a purchaser. The price was a little over £3000!

Jaguar kept the very last one for their own collection, which in recent times has been increased considerably.

C H A P T E R   S E V E N

THE
WORLD BEATING
XJ SALOONS

*The XJ saloons were Sir William
Lyons' finest achievement, and the
cars he prized most.*

uring the mid-sixties, the Jaguar company turned its thoughts towards rationalizing the saloon-car range. At that time there were 2.4, 3.4, and 3.8 Mark II's, 3.4 and 3.8 S-types, and the Mark X saloons. At the beginning of the decade Jaguar, needing space for expansion, had bought the Daimler company and acquired its Radford factory. Having also inherited a range of diverse vehicles, including luxurious, if dated, saloons, the SP250 sports car and commercial vehicles, Lyons diverted his energies to making a success at least of the buses and trucks. Rationalization was desperately needed, however, and Lyons had in mind a radical scheme to replace the lot with one car which other models might subsequently be based on and which could be powered by a range of engines.

Meanwhile, in 1964 the 4.2 engine was developed and fitted into the Mark X to sustain the model and improve its torque performance. Attention was also applied to the heating system and power steering. The all-synchromesh gearbox was now fitted to manual models and an improved Borg-Warner automatic transmission to 'shiftless' variants. This uprating maintained the car's popularity, particularly in the United States, where such a large car was not out of place.

♦ J A G U A R ♦
MARK X 4.2
SALOON & 420G

BODY STYLE(s): Large Saloon
ENGINE: XK Twin overhead cam
  6 cyl, 4235 cc
MAX POWER: 265 bhp
TIME: 0–60 10.4 secs
MAX SPEED: 122.5 mph
QUANTITY MADE: 5119
  (plus 18 Limousines) & 5739
  (plus 24 Limousines)
PRICE: £2199 & £2238
ANNOUNCEMENT DATE: Oct 1964 &
  Oct 1966
IN PRODUCTION: 1964–1966 & 1966–1970

♦ CONTEMPORARY COMPARISONS 1965 ♦

	MARK X	BUICK RIVIERA	ROLLS ROYCE SILVER CLOUD III	ROVER 3 LITRE	PONTIAC PARISIENNE	S TYPE
MAX SPEED	118	127	114	108	100	116
0–50	8.0	5.1	7.6	10.1	8.5	8.5
MPG	13.4	10.1	11.2	17.5	13.7	15.3
PRICE	£2199	£3929	£5632	£1708	£2430	£1945

	DAIMLER MAJESTIC MAJOR	HUMBER SUPER SNIPE	BRISTOL 408	VANDEN PLAS PRINCESS R	AUSTIN WEST-MINSTER	VAUXHALL CRESTA
MAX SPEED	122	98	125	112	102	97
0–50	7.1	12.0	7.0	9.1	10.4	7.2
MPG	16.0	15.8	15.0	15.4	17.5	17.0
PRICE	£2703	£1512	£4650	£1995	£998	£974

■ *In 1964 the Mark X saloon had its 3.8 engine replaced by a 4.2-litre version of the trusty XK unit. The unit was at the same time fitted to the E-type, but was specifically developed for the large and heavy saloon to improve performance.*

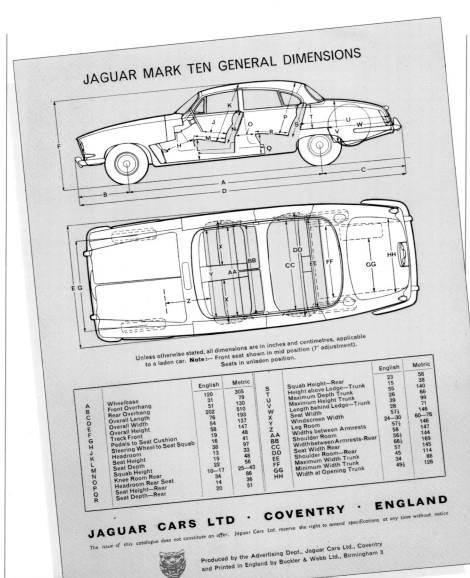

JAGUAR MARK TEN GENERAL DIMENSIONS

Unless otherwise stated, all dimensions are in inches and centimetres, applicable to a laden car. **Note :—** Front seat shown in mid position (7″ adjustment). Seats in unladen position.

		English	Metric
A	Wheelbase	120	305
B	Front Overhang	31	79
C	Rear Overhang	51	130
D	Overall Length	202	510
E	Overall Width	76	193
F	Overall Height	54	137
G	Track Front	58	147
H	Pedals to Seat Cushion	19	48
J	Steering Wheel to Seat Squab	16	41
K	Headroom	38	97
L	Seat Height	13	33
M	Seat Depth	19	48
N	Squab Height	22	56
O	Knee Room Rear Seat	10—17	25—43
P	Headroom Rear Seat	34	86
Q	Seat Height—Rear	14	36
R	Seat Depth—Rear	20	51

		English	Metric
S	Squab Height—Rear	23	58
T	Height above Ledge—Trunk	15	38
U	Maximum Depth Trunk	55	140
V	Maximum Height Trunk	26	66
W	Length behind Ledge—Trunk	39	99
X	Seat Width	28	71
Y	Windscreen Width	57½	146
Z	Leg Room	24—30	60—76
AA	Widths between Armrests	57½	146
BB	Shoulder Room	58	147
CC	Width between Armrests—Rear	56½	144
DD	Seat Width Rear	66½	169
EE	Shoulder Room—Rear	57	145
FF	Maximum Width Trunk	45	114
GG	Minimum Width Trunk	34	86
HH	Width at Opening Trunk	49½	126

JAGUAR CARS LTD · COVENTRY · ENGLAND

Produced by the Advertising Dept., Jaguar Cars Ltd., Coventry
and Printed in England by Buckler & Webb Ltd., Birmingham 3

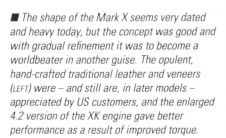

■ *The shape of the Mark X seems very dated and heavy today, but the concept was good and with gradual refinement it was to become a worldbeater in another guise. The opulent, hand-crafted traditional leather and veneers (LEFT) were – and still are, in later models – appreciated by US customers, and the enlarged 4.2 version of the XK engine gave better performance as a result of improved torque.*

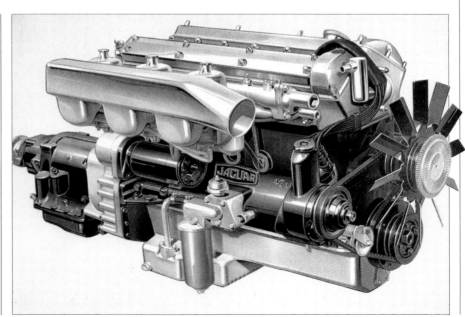

THE BMC MERGER

*O*n 29 July 1966, a document was issued detailing the proposed merger and formally offering Jaguar shareholders, of whom Lyons was the majority holder, the following:
(i) for each Ordinary Share of 5s. in Jaguar you are offered, credited as fully paid, two Ordinary Shares of 5s. and 22s. 6d. 8% Unsecured Loan Stock 1986/91 of B.M.C.;
(ii) for each A Ordinary Share of 5s. in Jaguar you are offered, credited as fully paid, two Ordinary Shares of 5s. and 10s. 3d. 8% Unsecured Loan Stock 1986/91 of B.M.C.

Lyons wrote under the heading, 'Advantages of the Merger': 'In writing this letter to you I must emphasise that I regard the merger as being in the best interests of your company – with rising costs, economies are becoming increasingly necessary to maintain profitability and the merger will provide the means to effect these economies.

'Other manufacturers throughout the world have recognised the need to take similar measures to achieve greater competitive power in finance, technology, manufacture and marketing, notably in America, France and Germany; a pattern which is now being followed in Japan.'

Jaguar profits were shown as follows for the five preceding years:

1961	2,061,773
1962	2,170,658
1963	2,252,744
1964	2,430,690
1965	2,434,273

The document, ironically, stated twice that, 'it has been agreed that Jaguar will continue to operate as a separate entity and with the greatest practicable degree of autonomy under the Chairmanship of Sir William Lyons'.

Sales of the S-types were disappointing and, with the new 'single' model still a year or so away, Lyons decided that an interim model was vital. Hence the 420 was introduced in 1967. In appearance it was an S-type with the Mark X frontal treatment. Like the S-type, it benefited from the independent rear suspension first fitted to the E-type but, unlike the S-type, it was fitted with the 4.2-litre engine. Like all Jaguars, it was generously praised by the press and the alterations to the front end seemed to make all the difference to sales, particularly in export markets. The Mark X, with its great bulbous sides, has tended to date in appearance; the 420, with its clue to future Lyons' thinking, has stood the test of time better. Being merely an interim model, it was produced only until the XJ6 was unveiled in 1968.

At the same time as the announcement of the 420, the Mark X changed its name (but little else) to the 420G. Outwardly distinguishable by the addition of a chrome strip running from front to rear at waist height, small flashers at the front end of the strip, the substitution of grilles for spotlights, and a larger centre slat to the main grille, it was mechanically unchanged. Inside, the dash top was given a padded roll as a safety feature, and in the centre of this roll was mounted a clock. What was termed a 'Limousine' version of the Mark X – with the addition of a glass screen dividing rear-seat

passengers from the driver, or perhaps one should say chauffeur – had been added to the range in 1964. The model continued with the renamed 420G until 1969. A year later, the 420G was finally dropped, having run concurrently with the XJ6 while supplies of the new car remained limited.

Lyons' son had been killed on the way to Le Mans in 1955 and so, apart from his two daughters, Lyons had no heir to his growing empire. He therefore took the decision in 1966 to merge his company with the giant British Motor Corporation (B.M.C.), manufacturers of Austin, Morris, M.G., Riley and Wolseley cars. It is now apparent that this was a most unfortunate decision which nearly brought the proud Jaguar company to extinction.

The merged company was known as British Motor Holdings and the idea was that the two concerns should operate quite autonomously. For two years this arrangement worked satisfactorily; the Chairman of B.M.C., Sir George Harriman, refrained from interfering in the Jaguar operations. The B.M.C. companies were running into financial problems, however, and when a predator in the shape of Leyland struck, the group, weakened by the B.M.C. element, was in no position to fight off Lord Stokes of Leyland. Thus, in 1968, the giant British Leyland was formed. It was then that problems really began.

■ *The 420, shown here with the Daimler version named the Sovereign in the foreground and the Jaguar model in the background sandwiching a 420G, was in essence an S-type with a revised frontal treatment and the larger 4.2-litre engine. It took the Mark X concept a stage further.*

♦ JAGUAR ♦
420 SALOON

BODY STYLE(s): Medium Sized Saloon
ENGINE: XK Twin overhead cam
  6 cyl, 4235 cc
MAX POWER: 245 bhp
TIME: 0–60 9.9 secs
MAX SPEED: 123 mph
QUANTITY MADE: 9600
PRICE: £1930
ANNOUNCEMENT DATE: Oct 1966
IN PRODUCTION: 1966–1968

In the same year the Mark II models, which had by then been in production for a considerable period, were revised with a view to keeping them going a little longer. The 3.8-litre model was dropped and the others became known as the 240 and 340. The appearance was modernized a little with slimmer bumpers; for reasons of economy leather hide was no longer used for the seats; and the spotlamps were replaced by grilles. The 2.4 engine benefited from some development and was fitted with a straight-port head similar to the E-type's. This resulted in an increase in power output from 120 bhp to 133 bhp. Solex carburettors were also replaced by ones of SU manufacture.

Soon after the fateful merger Jaguar announced the Daimler Limousine. Intended as a competitor to the Phantom Rolls Royces at a fraction of their price, it had a completely new and much larger bodyshell built on the Mark X floorpan and was fitted with the 4.2 engine. The Limousines have sold steadily over the years, especially overseas, and they are still made today, even though their basis, the Mark X/420G, went out of production in 1970 and the famous XK engine was finally replaced in 1986.

The year 1968 saw the appearance of Sir William Lyons' crowning achievement, the XJ6 saloon. It was not radically new, but a perfect blend and refinement of everything that was best in a Jaguar. What made it seem so different was that it was clothed in Lyons' styling *pièce de résistance*.

The project, codenamed XJ4, began in 1964 under the direction of Bill Heynes, and involved such men as Bob Knight and Tom Jones. Knight had built up a reputation second to none for achieving ride and handling allied to refinement.

♦**J A G U A R 2 4 0**♦
& 3 4 0 S A L O O N S

BODY STYLE(s): Compact Saloons
ENGINE: XK Twin overhead cam
6 cyl, 2483 & 3442 cc
MAX POWER: 133 bhp & 210 bhp
TIME: 0–60 12.5 secs & 8.8 secs
MAX SPEED: 106 mph & 124 mph
QUANTITY MADE: 4210 & 2630
PRICE: £1365 & £1442
ANNOUNCEMENT DATE: Sept 1967
IN PRODUCTION: 1967–1969 & 1967–1968

■ *BELOW In 1968 the Mark II models, by then a little long in the tooth, were renamed 240 and 340 and modernized in a few details. Jaguar was soon to adopt a policy of rationalization, concentrating on one saloon bodyshell, and in retrospect it is a pity that the company did not develop a successor to the Mark II's, for it abandoned a market that others, notably BMW, have captured to their profit.*

■ *RIGHT The Daimler Limousine became the company flagship.*

THE DAIMLER LIMOUSINE

There is one hall at the Browns Lane factory where small groups of men cluster round individual vehicles, their brows furrowed in concentration. These vehicles are of proportions distinctly different from any others in the factory. It is almost certain, furthermore, that no two will be the same. This is the Daimler Limousine Shop, where these stately, purpose-designed 'carriages' are built to order. There is no production line here; each vehicle is constructed from unpainted shell to final despatch by a small group of dedicated workers. Impractical for volume production, this method allows a long list of optional fitments to be built-in according to each customer's requirements. For example, the interior may be appointed in hand-stitched leather, knit-backed expanded vinyl or a choice of top-quality English cloths. The Daimler Limousine, still very much in production, is based on the Mark X floor pan and powered by the 4.2-litre XK engine. Indeed, with the introduction of the AJ6 engine into the latest XJ6 saloon range, it is the only use for the venerable XK unit.

The Limousine is exported all over the world, being one of the few cars still produced that was designed originally as a limousine.

It offers remarkable value for money in comparison with its few rivals. Daimler Limousines are used by many royal families and governments throughout the world, and as civic cars, chauffeur-driven hire fleets and large companies' courtesy cars.

Although left over from another age, the Daimler Limousines are keeping abreast of modern progress: on-board computers and communications technology allow them to be used as boardrooms on wheels.

Initially it was intended to use a 3-litre version of the six-cylinder XK engine and the new V12 engine when ready. However, the 3-litre did not possess the strong bottom-end torque which was a notable feature of all Jaguars and it was dropped in favour of the usual 4.2. Sir William was somewhat reluctant to use the taller 4.2, because it meant that he had to redesign the bonnet to make it larger. He felt, moreover, that the 4.2 was becoming rather old-fashioned. The engine was, as it turned out, destined to sustain Jaguar until 1986!

A new rear suspension was designed which, though similar in principle to the usual set-up, was mounted directly to the body. There were noise problems, however, and as time was pressing it was decided, rather at the last minute, to resort to the familiar system designed in the fifties and first seen in 1961.

When announced at the Royal Lancaster Hotel in London in September 1968, the XJ6 was accorded every possible accolade. It was voted 'Car of the Year' and won the 'Don Safety Award'. The press lavished praise on the new car for setting new standards in luxury, sporting motoring. They were impressed by the pre-eminent qualities of ride, handling, comfort, roadholding, style and uncanny silence. As usual the XJ6 offered unparalleled value for money. Lyons' cars had always been brilliantly cheap. Now they were also technically brilliant.

To describe the XJ6's shape as a compromise between the Mark X and the 420 would not do it justice. It was beautifully balanced and essentially modern, its feline, sporting look enhanced by the wide, low-profile radial tyres especially developed for the car by Dunlop.

The front suspension was given anti-dive characteristics by angling the wishbones and the engine was mounted directly to the front suspension sub-frame, which helped to insulate road noise. Rack and pinion steering, first adopted by the sports cars on the XK140, was finally adopted on the saloons. The dampers were no longer mounted inside the coil springs and the steering column was given a collapsible section. New, improved Girling brakes, with three-pot calipers at the front, had dual lines and a tandem master cylinder.

Alongside the familiar 4.2, a new 2.8-litre version of the faithful XK engine appeared at the announcement of the XJ6. In certain countries vehicle taxation was based on capacity and a 2.8 size promised worthwhile savings. Unfortunately it proved to be a troublesome engine and was discontinued in 1973.

■ On the way to the XJ6, Lyons tried a number of different designs. Illustrated here is one of the more extreme ideas – a very 'Italian' frontal treatment that is reminiscent of Bertone.

♦ J A G U A R   X J 6 ♦

BODY STYLE(s): Large Saloon
ENGINE: XK Twin overhead cam
  6 cyl, 2792 & 4235 cc
MAX POWER: 180 bhp & 245 bhp
TIME: 0–60 11 secs & 8.8 secs
MAX SPEED: 117 mph & 124 mph
QUANTITY MADE: 19,426 & 58,972
PRICE: £1797 & £2254
ANNOUNCEMENT DATE: Sept 1968
IN PRODUCTION: 1968–1973

As the orders flowed in and waiting lists became ever longer, a number of key people began to leave the stage. The seventies were to be a period of turmoil for Jaguar, as the British Leyland empire lurched from disaster to disaster, and successive changes of top management did little to bring stability to the group. At the end of 1968 Arthur Whittaker, Deputy Chairman, retired after a lifetime of devoted service. Rarely given the credit he deserves, he had played a vital part in the growth of the company from the very earliest days. A year later William Heynes C.B.E. retired as Vice-Chairman (Engineering). He had been responsible for every SS and Jaguar since 1935 and had built a team of engineers without peer in the British automotive industry. He was succeeded on the board by Wally Hassan and

■ *When the XJ6 arrived it received instant and widespread acclaim. The concept had been refined, it seemed, to perfection and Jaguar now had a saloon to rival, if not lead, the best in the world.*

Bob Knight, who had responsibility for power-unit and vehicle engineering respectively.

Wally Hassan had stayed on past the age of retirement to see the V12 engine successfully brought into production. The unit first appeared in the Series III E-types, but it was really intended for the commercially more important saloons.

In spite of the decision to produce a single-cam version rather than the twin-cam, the V12 was still a tight fit in the XJ bodyshell. With the machinations of the Leyland politics beginning to affect Jaguar, the introduction of the XJ12 was somewhat delayed and it was not until 1972, some four years after the XJ6 launch, that it was finally unleashed.

■ *Lyons' styling had reached its pinnacle and the Jaguar fortunes were to rest upon this model for nearly two decades. That it managed to sustain the company for so long proves how good the car was in 1968.*

WALTER 'WALLY' HASSAN

Wally Hassan, one of the great names of motor racing, had a fascinating career during which he played a significant part in the Jaguar story.

Apprenticed originally to Bentley Motors, he made a name for himself by tuning and building Brooklands cars. During this period he worked on a racing SS 100 for a customer and came into contact with Heynes.

When Heynes needed a chief experimental engineer, Hassan was his choice. With the outbreak of war and little on which to engage his fertile brain at SS, he moved to Bristol to work on carburettor development, but soon returned to Coventry when SS were given the task of designing a lightweight jeep for parachuting behind enemy lines. The results were the interesting little VA and VB machines with independent suspension and unitary construction.

Following the war, Hassan assisted with the design of the XK engine and the development of the XK120 before moving to fresh challenges at Coventry Climax. Here he designed the famous world-beating Grand Prix engines. When Climax was acquired by Jaguar, Hassan devoted his final working years to developing the V12 engine for production.

The praise was even more lavish than it had been in 1968. The XJ12 was considered a serious contender for the title, 'Best Car in the World', and was voted 'Car of the Year'. Just as it had been unheard-of to bring the complexity of a twin overhead camshaft engine within the realms of the man in the street – such a configuration had been reserved for racing engines in the late pre-war and early post-war days – so the sophisticated V12 configuration had been the province of racing cars and low-volume, Italian exotica. Jaguar had once more brought the height of sophistication to relatively large-scale production. There was arguably nothing to compare with the XJ12's quiet, silky-smooth, effortless power.

Great hopes were pinned on the V12. Large capital sums were invested in machinery, both to enable production to keep pace with the expected demand and to manufacture related versions such as a shortened V8 or a slant six. Jaguar could not know, indeed nobody could know, that the world

◆ **J A G U A R   X J 1 2** ◆

BODY STYLE(s): Large Saloon
ENGINE: V12 5343 cc
MAX POWER: 253 bhp
TIME: 0–60 7.4 secs
MAX SPEED: 146 mph
QUANTITY MADE: 3220
PRICE: £3726
ANNOUNCEMENT DATE: July 1972
IN PRODUCTION: 1972–1973

economy would be severely affected by a series of oil crises in the mid-seventies. At the beginning of the decade nobody gave much thought to fuel consumption. By its end the quest for economy had turned priorities upside down.

Externally the XJ12 was indistinguishable from the XJ6, apart from a different grille with a 'V' badge in the centre and an 'XJ12' on the vertical section of the bootlid. Ventilated discs helped to stop this car, which, with a maximum of 140 mph, was the fastest production four-seater available anywhere. With production affected by a long strike, the waiting lists were ridiculously long – that is, until the first fuel crisis.

After a long and highly distinguished career, Wally Hassan took

■ *Jaguar had difficulty in meeting demand for the XJ6, and when the V12-engined version, the XJ12, arrived, the waiting lists became excessive. The XJ12 had the superb styling, refinement and roadholding of its 6-cylinder sister, and it was even more silent and more effortlessly powerful.*

retirement in 1972 and was succeeded by his deputy, Harry Mundy. In the same year Lyons, having reached the age of 70, retired and handed over the reins of 'his' company to Lofty England, who became Chairman and Chief Executive.

In 1972 long-wheelbase versions of the XJ6 and XJ12 made their debut at the Frankfurt Motor Show. One of the few criticisms of the XJ had been its poor rear legroom and its awkward accessibility for rear passengers. These deficiencies were overcome by the introduction of the long wheelbase and although at first both models were sold, the shorter-wheelbase model was soon dropped.

The Frankfurt Show in September 1973 saw the introduction of the Series II XJ's. The engineers under Knight, who had assumed total

■ One of the very few criticisms of the XJ models was the poor rear access and the lack of rear legroom. To overcome this, long-wheelbase versions joined the range and eventually dislodged the original models. The XJ12 models were distinguished by an appropriate script on the rear and an altered grille with V12 badge at the front.

responsibility for engineering, had improved various details. Attention was paid to the heating, ventilating and air-conditioning systems. The dash layout was considerably revised so that the minor instruments, which had formerly occupied the centre, were now clustered around the main speedo and rev counter in front of the driver. The switching was altered to allow a number of functions to be operated by the stalk controls attached to the steering column.

The major differences, which were immediately noticeable, were external. Because of impending US regulations, the front bumper height had to be raised, which meant that a new, more shallow, grille had to be designed. Below the bumper was a further rectangular grille. The rear remained unchanged apart from the number plate light, which was moved

from the bumper to a position above the number plate.

Announced concurrently with the Series II cars at Frankfurt were two new models. The XJC's, more often known as the XJ Coupes, were two-door versions of the short-wheelbase XJ saloon. With no pillar behind the door to break the line, the windows could be lowered out of sight, leaving the whole side completely open. This made for a most stylish car and it is not surprising that the Coupe was a great favourite of Sir William.

Production was delayed by problems with side-window sealing and difficulties in maintaining a level of wind noise low enough to be acceptable on a Jaguar. Only a comparatively small number of Coupes was made before they were killed off as a result of the short-wheelbase configuration's being dropped for the saloon.

In September 1973 Lord Stokes appointed an outsider, Geoffrey Robinson, to the position of Managing Director. Since May 1972 Robinson had been running the Innocenti plant in Italy where Minis were produced. A few months later Lofty England retired and went to live in Austria.

In late 1974 the ailing British Leyland was taken under the government's wing and nationalized. Sir Donald Ryder was commissioned to prepare a report on the company. The Ryder Report advocated that the company's

■ The Series II XJ models incorporated a number of improvements to meet American regulations. The most noticeable of the external changes was the raising of the front bumper height, with a new grille above and supplementary one below the new bumper.

♦ **JAGUAR XJ6 &** ♦
XJ12 SERIES II

BODY STYLE(s): Large Saloon
ENGINE: XK 6 cyl, 4235 cc & V12 5343 cc
MAX POWER: 170 bhp & 285 bhp
TIME: 0–60 8.8 secs & 7.8 secs
MAX SPEED: 124 mph & 147 mph
QUANTITY MADE: 77,501 & 16,060
PRICE: £3674 & £4702
ANNOUNCEMENT DATE: Sept 1973
IN PRODUCTION: 1973–1979

management and technical functions be centralized rather than devolved, as they were at the time, to each company or factory. This change probably hurt the fiercely proud and independent Jaguar most, especially since Jaguar had been contributing substantial profits to the unwieldy empire. The Jaguar Board was disbanded and Robinson departed.

The only department in the whole group which escaped the new centralization was Jaguar Engineering, where Bob Knight fought tooth and nail to maintain the department within the Browns Lane factory and under his control. A number of present senior Jaguar personnel believe that had he failed, and Engineering been lost, it is unlikely that Jaguar would have survived to make its miraculous recovery of the eighties.

♦ J A G U A R ♦
X J 6 C & X J 1 2 C

BODY STYLE(s): Two Door Coupes
ENGINE: XK 6 cyl, 4235 cc & V12 5343 cc
MAX POWER: 245 bhp & 285 bhp
TIME: 0–60 8.8 secs & 7.8 secs
MAX SPEED: 124 mph & 148 mph
QUANTITY MADE: 6541 & 1862
PRICE: £4260 & £5181
ANNOUNCEMENT DATE: Sept 1973
IN PRODUCTION: 1974–1977

■ *LEFT AND BELOW The absence of a 'B'-post window pillar produced an extremely graceful and stylish effect when the windows were lowered out of sight. The rear windows worked on a crank in order to avoid the rear wheel arches. On the XJC's the roofs were finished in a vinyl trim, which added to the sporty appearance.*

■ *LEFT The additional models introduced in 1973 were known as the XJ Coupes. Their two doors and pillarless construction made them especially attractive. The V12 versions of the Daimler XJ's were known as Double Sixes. Illustrated (above left) are a Coupe and a vintage Daimler Double Six.*

While the company was being reorganized, thought was being given to an XJ6 replacement, and throughout the decade a number of styling exercises were attempted as the team, led by Knight, grappled with the unenviable task of following Lyons. Their efforts were hampered by a lack of money within the group and by constant changes of top management, but even in this unhealthy climate, the XJ-S was unveiled in 1975.

Jaguar's policy was to share as many components between models as possible, rather than maintain a plethora of different concepts in production as in the previous decade. Thus the XJ-S used a version of the short-wheelbase saloon floorpan and had basically saloon suspension. Fitted with the V12 engine and a closed two-door sporting body, the XJ-S was a grand

ABOVE In spite of modern technology, the Jaguar company retains many pre-war traditions and employs highly skilled craftsmen in what is the largest trim shop in Europe. Body manufacture and painting (CENTRE RIGHT) is carried out at the Castle Bromwich plant in Birmingham. The Browns Lane factory (ABOVE RIGHT) was for many years Jaguar's only plant, but despite being considerably expanded, it is now just one of four plants in the Midlands. Browns Lane still houses the main offices and the three production lines (BOTTOM RIGHT) on which the cars are assembled.

touring car rather than a sports car. It was certainly no E-type and opinion remains divided with regard to the styling. There was, however, no question about its technical merit, with the superb V12 engine at the heart. The V12 was fitted with Lucas fuel injection and gave the XJ-S 150-mph performance. The long bonnet rather reminded one of Lyons' earlier creations, but now the space under it was very full! The XJ-S was a car to take on the Italian exotica at a fraction of the price and it had the usual high standards of Jaguar refinement that few, if any, rivals could match in so fast a car.

A period of comparative stability came to BL (as it was renamed after the Ryder Report) when Michael Edwardes was brought in as Chairman to sort the company out. This he proceeded to do and he was knighted for his Herculean efforts. One of his first acts was to make Bob Knight Managing Director of Jaguar and to allow a fair degree of autonomy again. Unlike Ryder, he understood that names such as Jaguar were some of Great Britain's greatest assets and that individual identity should be encouraged, rather than submerged. Certain functions remained centralized, even so, and out of Jaguar's control.

As a result Jaguar received consistently inferior components from several major suppliers and quite unbelievably poor bodies and paintwork from BL's Castle Bromwich plant, which assembled the Jaguar bodies and over which Jaguar had no control. Knight tried to act where he could and appointed David Fielden as Quality Director. But Jaguar quality took a dive.

With the replacement XJ40, as the car was termed within Jaguar, still some way off, the decision was taken to replace the Series II with a rather more radically altered Series III. The small styling department at Jaguar was fully committed to the new car and the well known Italian firm, Pininfarina, was contracted to carry out a styling update. This work, with final modifications at Jaguar, resulted in a car that was subtly altered but cleverly modernized. The roof was the main area to be altered. It became flatter, improving rear headroom and allowing the fitting of a sunshine roof. The windscreen rake was increased and the front and rear screens were glued in, giving greater strength to the body. Minor changes included the fitting of

BOB KNIGHT

Bob Knight went to work for Jaguar in the forties and specialized initially in chassis work. He was the project engineer for the C-type and became one of the world's most eminent development engineers.

While refining the unitary-construction Mark I saloons he used rubber mountings to good effect, damping out much unwelcome noise and vibration. This was to become something of a speciality and he is often remembered for his pre-eminent ride and refinement work. No better example exists of his work in this field than the ultra-silent, smooth XJ saloons that set new standards when they were introduced in 1968.

He worked in conjunction with Bill Heynes, developing a number of his ideas. In the mid-fifties he designed the independent rear suspension first seen on the E-type and used on every Jaguar up to the XJ40 During the troubled seventies, he fought long and hard for Jaguar independence and autonomy within the British Leyland empire. He succeeded in keeping the Jaguar engineering department intact when every other department in every other BL company was centralized and this achievement is hailed by many as vital to the survival of Jaguar. Later he was appointed Managing Director by Sir Michael Edwardes. He retired in 1980.

GROUP 44 TRANS AM

*G*roup 44 had been running the aging V12 E-type in US races with excellent results and so it was natural that, when the XJ-S arrived, they were keen to carry on. An XJ-S was therefore prepared for the Trans Am series and given an exploratory outing in August 1976. The basically standard suspension was stiffened up and ventilated discs were fitted at the rear. The diff fluid was kept from boiling as a result of heat soak by pumping it through a small rear-mounted oil cooler. With six Weber carburettors replacing the Bosch fuel injection of the production car and other tuning as applied to the previous racing E-types, the power output was in the region of 530/540 bhp.

The modified XJ-S was slower than the Group 44 E-type in a straight line, but handling was improved. Team leader, Bob Tullius, scored four wins during 1977 and also a second place, a third and a fourth. These results were just sufficient to give him the title of Category 1 Champion.

A new, lightened car was built for 1978 and power was increased to 560 bhp, thus keeping it competitive against the mass of Corvettes, which were lighter but a little less powerful. The Corvettes took the first three rounds, but Tullius pulled the XJ-S and his points score past the Chevrolets. A class win and seventh overall in the six-hour World Championship of Makes round at Watkins Glen was one of the more notable results. With Tullius assured of the driver's title for a second year, a second XJ-S, in fact the 1977 car, was entered by the team to try to take the manufacturer's title for Jaguar from the overwhelming number of Corvettes. They succeeded!

flush exterior door handles, a cleaner arrangement of rear lights and a new grille.

The large and unsightly black rubber bumpers, which had been fitted on all US export Series II models, now appeared as standard on the **Series III**. When built for the United States, they incorporated 5-mph impact-absorbing beams. A 3.4-litre version had been introduced in 1975 and now that version and the 4.2-litre could be ordered with five-speed gearboxes. Fuel injection was now fitted to the 4.2 which, with enlarged inlet valves, produced an extra 30 bhp.

The revisions, once the quality problems were eventually sorted out, were extremely favourably received and the Series III XJ sustained the company's fortunes considerably longer than was ever intended.

♦ J A G U A R   X J S ♦

BODY STYLE(s): Two Door Closed Coupe
ENGINE: V12 5343 cc
MAX POWER: 285 bhp
TIME: 0–60 6.7 secs
MAX SPEED: 153 mph
QUANTITY MADE: 14792
PRICE: £8900
ANNOUNCEMENT DATE: Sept 1975
IN PRODUCTION: 1975–1981

♦ J A G U A R ♦
X J   3 . 4 ,   4 . 2   &   5 . 3
S A L O O N S   S E R I E S   I I I

BODY STYLE(s): Large Saloon
ENGINE: XK 6 cyl, 3442 cc,
  4235 cc & V12 5343 cc
MAX POWER: 162 bhp, 205 bhp & 296 bhp
TIME: 0–60 10.9 secs, 10.5 secs & 7.4 secs
MAX SPEED: 117 mph, 128 mph & 147 mph
QUANTITY MADE: 5760, 150,203 &
  still in production
PRICE: £11,189, £12,326 & £15,014
ANNOUNCEMENT DATE: March 1979
IN PRODUCTION: 1979–1986
  1979–1986 & 1979

■ *BELOW The subtly, but effectively, restyled Series III XJ saloons restored the company's fortunes after the ravages of BL management and the appalling quality problems which came with it.*

■ *ABOVE In 1975 the E-type's so-called replacement finally arrived. To many people it was a disappointment. Based on the saloon mechanics, with a body of questionable design, it was a superb, silent, high-speed express, but it was no sports car!*

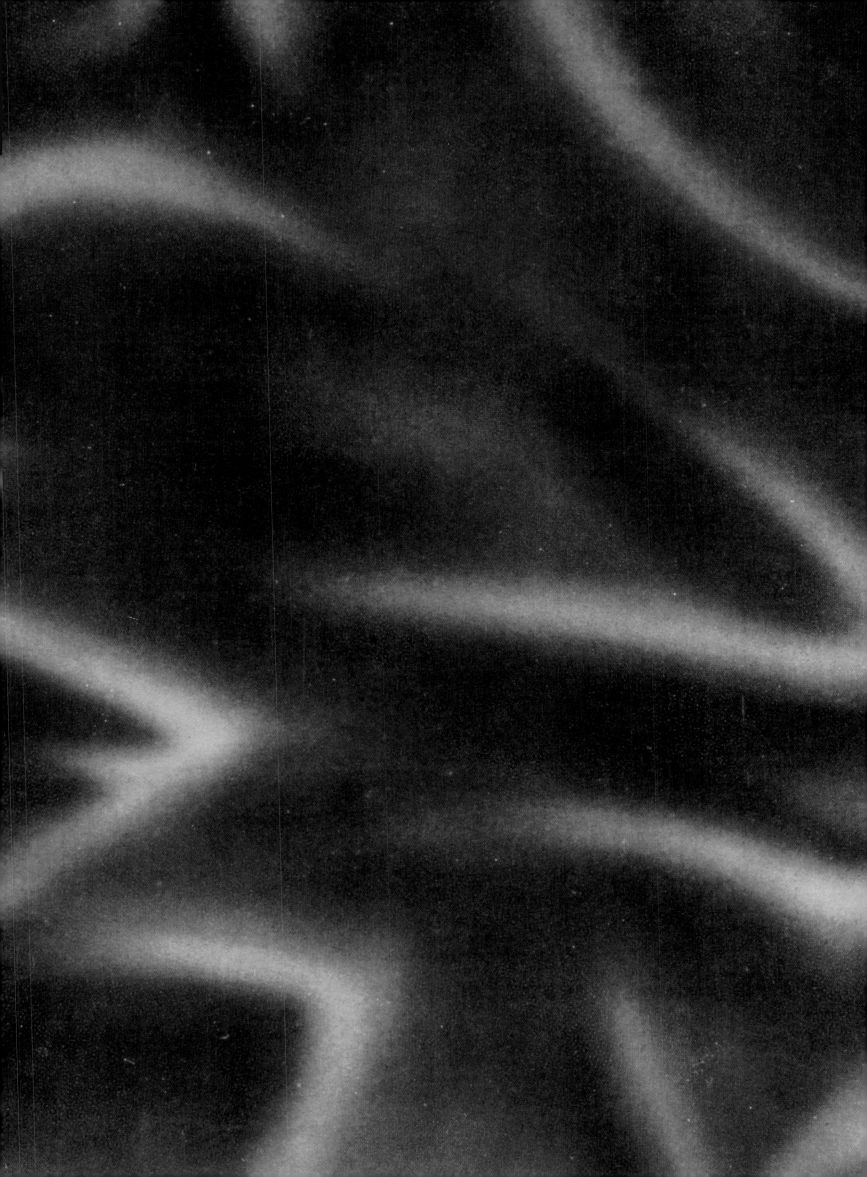

CHAPTER EIGHT

THE LEGEND IS REBORN

The car upon which the fortunes of Jaguar will rest in the 1990s, the new XJ6, was the first to be designed after Sir William Lyons' retirement.

*I*n 1980 Sir Michael Edwardes offered the position of full-time Jaguar Chairman to John Egan and, after long and careful deliberation, Egan accepted the challenge. Bob Knight, always an engineer at heart, had struggled valiantly with the problems created by 'big brother' during his period as Managing Director. He had put together a fine management team, many of whom were to play a vital role in the eighties. Like so many loyal and devoted Jaguar men, he had given his life to the company. But in July he retired, leaving his successors to take up where he left off.

A strike was in progress when Egan joined the company. A succession of part-time outside Chairmen had done little for morale, but somehow Egan convinced the shop stewards of his determination and by a small margin the men voted to return to work. It was the first of many successes for the new 'boss'.

In the earlier seventies production had been up around 30,000 vehicles per annum, but by 1980 successive fuel crises and the Castle Bromwich problems had helped to reduce the number to under 14,000. The company was losing more than £40m a year on a turnover of only £150m. There was, however, one encouraging sign. Just before he retired, Knight had been offered control of the Castle Bromwich body plant; Egan was thus able to tackle one of the major stumbling blocks to higher production and improved quality.

Egan saw quality as the key to rebuilding Jaguar's fortunes. He was ruthless with the suppliers and blunt with the BL hierarchy. The problems of Castle Bromwich were tackled and production began to increase. With effective P.R., the message began to get around that quality was improving. In the United States it had become a joke that you needed two Jaguars – one to run while the other was in the garage! But the new Jaguar management showed that it could act effectively. It announced that owners of the company's cars would be contacted and their experiences with their new Jaguar monitored. This made news.

With little money to spare and the problems with the present products to tackle, it is hardly surprising that progress with the XJ40 was slow. Throughout the seventies, a small team under Knight had been working away to produce a large number of mock-ups in an attempt to find a design for the XJ6's successor. Certain members of BL's management felt that the XJ was old-fashioned and that the new car must be radically different. A number of Germanic box-like creations were, therefore tried. Eventually, however, the day was carried by the argument that a Jaguar was distinctively a Jaguar and must above all be stylish. Following in Knight's footsteps was an unenviable task. He had created every production Jaguar except the E-type and was acknowledged as one of the very finest automotive designers the world had seen. For that reason (though customer preference was also borne in mind) it was decided the XJ40 should be evolutionary, not revolutionary.

A mock-up of the new style achieved a higher score at a BL styling clinic than any other had ever achieved throughout the group. This must have helped Egan to persuade the BL board and the Conservative government that it was worth 'risking' a further £100m on Jaguar.

The thirsty V12 engine was given a new lease of life in 1981 with the adoption of new cylinder heads which incorporated principles developed by a Swiss engineer named Michael May. The May Fireball combustion

■ *During the 1970s and early 1980s Jaguar management experimented with a series of very different mock-ups in an effort to design a worthy successor to the XJ saloons. One school of thought felt that the XJs were old-fashioned and that the new Jaguar should be a more Germanic, box-like creation. Thankfully, stronger pro-Jaguar forces prevailed.*

SIR JOHN EGAN

When Sir William retired in 1972, Jaguar was just entering its traumatic British Leyland spell. Having lost his son in a motoring accident in 1955, he had no male heir and though Lofty England was the natural successor, he, too, was not far from retirement age. Apart from Bob Knight, a number of outside men were brought in by BL and they held various positions of authority but without success. In 1980 Sir Michael Edwardes appointed John Egan to the post of Jaguar Chairman. Egan had enjoyed success within BL when he set up the Unipart spare parts operation, but had left the group to join Massey Ferguson. He was tempted back by the challenge, believing, after long reflection, that Jaguar had a 50/50 chance of survival. Inheriting an excellent team, he and Mike Beasley, who was to become Assistant Managing Director, set about Jaguar's awful quality problems.

They were ruthless with the suppliers, who had been the cause of so many of the problems, and, with good P.R., managed to persuade the car-buying public that Jaguars were once again reliable cars.

This new image was reflected in increased sales and, together with increased productivity, brought about a return to profits. Jaguar's once-tarnished image was restored and Jaguar became once more the flagship of the British motor industry. In recognition of this fine achievement, Egan was knighted in 1986.

chamber benefited from lean-burn characteristics. Inlet and exhaust valves were set at different levels and by this means, together with a ramped interconnecting channel, the fuel mixture was induced to swirl around. This turbulence had the beneficial effect of making the normally slow-igniting, very lean fuel mixtures burn rapidly and completely. The result was greater fuel economy. Jaguar was the first to adopt and successfully develop these principles, though other manufacturers had worked along similar lines. The new engine was termed HE, which stood for 'high efficiency'.

In 1981 the HE engine was introduced into the range and fitted to the XJ saloon and XJ-S. The saloon, now known as the XJ12 HE, was at the same time given alloy wheels, a headlamp wash/wipe, electrically-operated door mirrors and sunshine roof. Consumption improved around twenty per cent, the car giving 26.8 mpg at 56 mph and 15mpg for the 'Urban Cycle".

For such a fast, heavy and, above all, refined car this was very respectable. The V12's continued to sell well in continental Europe, especially in Germany, where, without the hindrance of speed limits, the 5.3 litres of V12 engine could be used to the maximum.

Production of the XJ-S actually ceased for a while and BL tried to kill it off for good. Egan, however, was convinced that BL was wrong and said so. Sales began to revive as the quality message spread and with the arrival of the HE engine the sales graph continued upwards. Whatever one's opinion as to the looks of the car, there was no denying that few other cars in the world were capable of carrying their occupants at over 150 mph in comparative silence while returning 22 mpg at 75 mph. The XJ-S was no sports car, but it served as an admirable executive's express. In the United States it found favour with the ladies as an alternative to the sporting Mercedes.

Coincident with the advent of the HE engine, some other changes were made to the XJ-S. The appearance was improved by the chroming of the

■ *ABOVE* *Production of the XJ-S ceased for a while, but improved quality and the more economical HE version of the V12 engine revived flagging sales. The model accounted for around a quarter of total Jaguar sales.*

■ *LEFT* *The Series III XJ saloons sustained the company and returned it to profitability, allowing the government to privatize Jaguar once more and giving the engineers the time to make sure the XJ40, as the new car was codenamed, would be right.*

THE RETURN OF GROUP 44

Group 44 returned to the Trans Am fray in 1981 with a more heavily modified XJ-S. The rules now allowed far more changes to be made to the standard car and the monocoque was replaced by a space-frame chassis. The engine and transmission were set well back in an effort to eliminate wheelspin.

The 1981 season was not so successful as the earlier ones, but Tuilus did, in fact, score more wins than the eventual champion. Unfortunately, retirements prevented him from backing up his two wins with consistent places.

■ ABOVE The XJ-S was popular with ladies who lived the 'Dallas' lifestyle in the United States and it challenged the sports Mercedes, so long a favourite of that set. Mercedes Benz, (and to a lesser extent BMW and Porsche) is perceived as Jaguar's main competition.

■ RIGHT In 1984 Jaguar once more had a presence at Le Mans when Group 44 designed, built and entered a sports prototype powered by the V12 engine. The car was successful in neither France nor the United States.

bumper blade above the black rubber monstrosities, helping to disguise
them a little. Other cosmetic changes included the fitting of a circular bonnet
badge; and the side was graced with a double coachline. Alloy wheels, the
return of a veneered dash, greater use of leather, new Dunlop tyres and a
microcomputer-based stereo system completed the modifications.

Production improved a little in 1981 to 14,577 and the company returned
to profit in the second half of the year. The following 12 months saw a very
healthy jump to a production figure of 22,046. Sales, which had been
running at just over 6,000 in the United States in 1976, had fallen to a
fraction over 3,000 by 1980, but by 1982 had revived to over 10,000.

Tom Walkinshaw Racing, often known simply as TWR, had been making
a name for itself racing production cars and in 1982 it was commissioned to
construct an XJ-S for racing in Australia. From this commission emerged the
idea that such a machine would be capable of taking on the dominant BMW's
in the European Touring Championship. From their debut in mid-season,
they took four wins, including a nostalgic one-two in the Tourist Trophy,
which Jaguar had not won since Stirling Moss' victory in a C-type in 1951.

With economy in mind, power output was 'restricted' to 400 bhp, but this
gave the racing XJ-S's a top speed in the order of 170 mph. The full season
in 1983 yielded encouraging results, though the sheer weight of numbers
made the task no easy one. The two Jaguars were competing against more
than a dozen BMW's who had the additional advantage of several years'
experience at the game. The season ended with BMW taking six wins and
Jaguar just one fewer.

During 1982 Group 44 decided, with Jaguar backing, to harness the V12
engine, about which they now knew a great deal, to a specially-designed

PRIVATIZATION

*O*ne national British newspaper
headlined it as the '£3
BILLION STAMPEDE' as investors
and speculators rushed to acquire
Jaguar shares following the
Conservative government's decision
to sell off Jaguar and return it to
private ownership once more.
There were well over 300,000
applications for varying amounts of
the 178 million shares, which were
offered at £1.65 each. The offer was
nearly 10 times over-subscribed,
leaving many disappointed.
There was pandemonium at
Barclays Bank City branch on the
final morning for applications, as
more than a thousand people tried
to beat the 10 a.m. deadline. Boxes
of forms were thrown over the
crowd and the traffic in the street
outside was brought to a halt by
would-be investors' cars. One
stockbroker left his taxi in a traffic
jam and ran several hundred yards
to the bank with only minutes to
spare. Others were less lucky. The
sale was also popular with German
investors and the company's
workforce, who were given 300
shares each, purchased £3.5m worth
additionally. Since the flotation,
the shares have enjoyed solid
international support and by early
1987, the share price had risen to
more than £6.00.

prototype sports racing car. The intention was to develop the car gradually, competing in IMSA events in the United States, with a long term aim of taking Jaguar back to Le Mans.

Lee Dykestra designed a good-looking, closed body and an aluminium honeycomb monocoque with steel bulkheads. The design contained an element of ground effect, then popular and still allowed in Formula One. As in the XJ13, the engine was employed as a stressed member and to it was attached the rear suspension. Several wins were notched up in 1983, though other people's accidents and minor faults did not help.

Although the V12 engine had been given a new lease of life, the XK was getting a little long in the tooth. The engine was never meant to remain in production for so long. It had been envisaged that the path to progress would be to manufacture smaller engine variations on the V12 tooling. It was not to be. The V8 that was built suffered from vibration problems and, though they were eventually overcome, the unit sounded like a four-cylinder – definitely not right for a Jaguar. Half a V12 was considered next, but the resulting 'slant six' lacked power. Thoughts of competition were, at any rate, surfacing again and a four-valve head was designed and fitted to the V12.

A similar head was tried on the XK engine and might well have been successful, but it was felt that this engine, designed in the 1940's, had several areas, for example crankshaft-sealing, that needed tackling by means of a complete redesign. Apart from anything else, economy was becoming vital and weight took on a new significance. The XK was a very heavy engine.

The May principles worked well when applied to the V12 and so it was decided that the best of both worlds would be to design a completely new, all-aluminium engine that could be offered in two versions. The performance version would have the four-valve head and the economy version would have one V12 HE head. The new six-cylinder had to have the same cylinder bore centres as the twelve to allow the existing machinery to be utilized for machining heads.

The new engine was called the AJ6, which stood for Advanced Jaguar six-cylinder. Like the XK engine in the XK120, and the V12 engine in the E-type, the new engine was first seen in the lower-volume sporting car.

In 1984 the AJ6 in 3.6-litre form with the 24-valve head was introduced in the model known as the XJ-S 3.6. With its manual gearbox, a five-speed Getrag, and more noticeable engine note the new car reminded one a little of the E-type. Externally, the new model was immediately distinguishable by its large bonnet bulge, which was necessary to incorporate the higher engine.

Of more interest to many was the new additional model which appeared at the same time. This was actually an open car though it was not a full convertible, because the manufacturers had assumed, erroneously, that American regulations would ban open cars in the future. It had no folding hood, but the 'cabriolet' top had removable roof panels and a folding rear window.

A firm called Lynx Engineering, which had made a name for itself by restoring and building superb replicas of the D-type, had taken the lead and offered a fully-convertible XJ-S some time before. Jaguar's own version, the XJ-SC, was fitted only with the new 3.6 and thus had the same bonnet bulge as the Coupe. Owing to safety regulations, the two small rear seats were removed; the open car was strictly a two-seater. The split roof allowed one to lift off the panel over the driver only, or over the passenger, or both. The

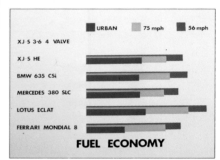

♦ **J A G U A R** ♦
XJ–S 3.6, XJ–SC 3.6,
XJ–S HE & XJ–SC HE

BODY STYLE(s): Two Door Closed Coupe & Cabriolets
ENGINE: AJ6 24 valve 3590 cc & V12 5343 cc
MAX POWER: 225 bhp & 295 bhp
TIME: 0–60 7.6 secs (all)
MAX SPEED: 145 mph, 142 mph, 148 mph & 150 mph
QUANTITY MADE: Still in production
PRICE: £19,249, £20,756, £21,753 & £26,995
ANNOUNCEMENT DATE: Oct 1983, Oct 1983, 1981 & July 1985
IN PRODUCTION: 1984 – & 1981 –

	■ URBAN	75 mph	■ 56 mph
XJ-S 3-6 4 VALVE			
XJ-S HE			
BMW 635 CSi			
MERCEDES 380 SLC			
LOTUS ECLAT			
FERRARI MONDIAL 8			

FUEL ECONOMY

■ *ABOVE As successive fuel crises made fuel consumption of greater importance, Jaguar were not well placed with their large, thirsty engines and heavy, refined cars. The engineers therefore developed the HE version of the V12 and began designing a new lightweight 6-cylinder engine for the new saloon range.*

■ *RIGHT Like the XK and V12 engines, the new AJ6 engine was introduced in a comparatively low-volume sports model, the sporting XJ-S. The new unit, with a four-valve head, gave good performance and reasonable economy. At the same time as the new engine was offered in the coupe, an open Cabriolet version of the XJ-S was added to the range.*

XJR-6 DESIGN

*I*n late 1984, the author spoke to designer Tony Southgate about the philosophy behind the design of the XJR-6 and what he had set out to achieve.

'The idea of the Jaguar is to take advantage of the weak areas of the Porsche. Although the Porsche is a "ground effect" car and the highest downthrust car they have ever produced, by Formula One standards it is quite modest. So I set out to design a body shape to produce maximum downforce with acceptable drag. At slower circuits you can tolerate a lot more drag and go for maximum downthrust. In that form, with 600 bhp available, it will do around 185 mph. The monocoque and body are made of carbon fibre, which has replaced good old aluminium, being much more rigid and quite light. The Jaguar engine is very heavy and very high; so I went to great lengths to cram the engine forward. It's recessed into the bulkhead, right close to the driver's shoulder in an attempt to get the weight as far forward as possible . . . The suspension at the front is a push-rod, rocker type system. The gearbox is a March one, as used on their Indianapolis and IMSA cars. We are making changes all the time. There is a steady list. All we need is a bit of time to clean it up and make some lighter ones.'

removed panels could then be stowed in a bag in the boot. One had a choice at the rear of either a 'solid' heated rear window or a lined folding hood and window which extended from the rollover bar rearwards. Aston Martin Tickford modified the original coupe body to produce the Cabriolet. With its manual gearbox, lively performance, fresh-air capability and good economy, the Cabriolet was in great demand.

In 1984 TWR added a third XJ-S to its strength and set about ending BMW's domination of racing. It won five of its first six races, with victories at Monza in Italy, Donington in England, Perguso near Enna in central Sicily, Brno in Czechoslovakia and Zeltweg in Austria. First place followed at the Salzburgring in Austria and a good win was scored in the Spa 24-hour classic in Belgium. The result of all this was that the title of European Touring Car Champion went to team leader, Tom Walkinshaw. The Jaguars had dominated.

At Le Mans that year Jaguar, in the shape of Group 44, had returned to its old hunting ground. It was not a particularly auspicious return, but nothing miraculous was expected and it was emphasized by all concerned that this was merely an exploratory outing.

The company was presented with the coveted Queen's Award to Industry in April, and a month later it was announced in parliament that Jaguar was to be sold off to the public. For Jaguar, this meant autonomy once more, which was what John Egan had been pressing for and what Sir William, now in his 83rd year, wanted.

After the XJ-S's successes in European events, the cars were retired and TWR graduated to international sports car racing. Former Grand Prix designer, Tony Southgate, was retained to pencil a state-of-the-art machine which could take on the might of Porsche. The resulting car, built of composite honeycomb and Kevlar, was one of the most effective yet in terms of ground effect efficiency. With their smaller turbocharged engines, the Porsches had more outright power than the Jaguars and their drivers could

■ *ABOVE AND TOP RIGHT Tom Walkinshaw Racing (TWR) began racing an XJ-S and in 1984 the team took seven wins against the hordes of BMWs and gave Walkinshaw the European Touring Car Championship.*

■ *RIGHT The British TWR team graduated, like Group 44 in the United States, to designing, building and entering a sports prototype based on the V12 engine.*

turn up the boost on their turboes for qualifying and overtaking. It was, therefore, essential that the XJR-6's had the best possible chassis and suspension. These were the areas in which Great Britain led the world in Grand Prix racing and at Indianapolis.

With the ultra-effective ground effect design, which had the effect of exerting tremendous downforce on the car and, as it were, 'gluing' it to the road, the TWR team would pray for rain when roadholding rather than straightline speed came into its own! The TWR XJR-6's were not considered ready for Le Mans and Group 44 again entered a brace of XJR-5's. Unfortunately, neither fared well.

In July 1985 the Cabriolet became available with a V12 engine. With Lucas-Bosch Digital Electronic fuel injection, the power-unit produced a shade under 300 bhp, giving the car a top speed of 150 mph and a capability of reaching 60 mph from standstill in just seven seconds. While the Cabriolet may be a less efficient shape aerodynamically, it is considered by many to be considerably more pleasing without the controversial rear 'flying buttresses' of the closed version.

In terms of refinement, that essential Jaguar quality, the 3.6-litre engine had not been too enthusiastically received by the press. Fitting it in the same body as the V12, which it could never hope to match in refinement, allowed a direct, if unfair, comparison to be made and the engine was a little noisy. Attention was paid to this, as the engine designed with the XJ40 primarily in mind had to be absolutely right for that model's launch.

Jaguar, now independent, was under less pressure to release the new model. When Egan and his colleagues had originally 'sold' the project to the BL board, they had had to pretend that they would be ready to launch it in 1984. In reality, there were problems which took time to solve and every major manufacturer takes at least six years to develop a completely new design at this level of complexity. Jaguar could afford to wait. The XJ saloons belied their age and were selling well. In fact, demand was greater than supply.

The three TWR XJ-S's were brought out of retirement in October and taken to Australia, where they took part in the classic saloon car race down under, the James Hardie 1000 at Bathurst. The long trip was worthwhile, as

At Brands Hatch in 1984, the author spoke to two members of the TWR driving strength, Jan Lammers, sometime Formula One driver and highly experienced sports car racer, and Alan Jones, the Australian former world champion. Both had driven the rival Porsches.

Jan Lammers commented that 'the Jaguar is a lot nicer to drive from the driver's point of view because it is a lot more pleasant to drive without a turbo. With the turbo, you've got an enormous amount of throttle lag which makes it difficult to set the car up. This engine is so precise.'

Jones agreed. 'It's a much better chassis – no question about that. It hasn't got so much horsepower because with the old Porsche having a turbo you can just lean over and dial the horsepower in. But chassis-wise, brake-wise and gearbox-wise, it's much nicer than the Porsche. I've nothing against the engine, it's very smooth but without the turbo boost, it's just not putting out so many gee-gees!'

■ *ABOVE LEFT Demand for the chic Cabriolet version of the XJ-S outstripped supply and in 1985 the V12 was offered as well as the new six.*

■ *RIGHT The Porsches, rich in experience and deep in numbers, retained their stranglehold on Group C racing, but the XJR-6s were constantly improving.*

■ *OPPOSITE AND ABOVE Teamwork at Brands Hatch, 1985: Alan Jones, Jan Lammers and Hans Heyer (top left, from left to right) drove the two XJR-6s. They found the normally aspirated V12-engined car easier to drive than the turbo-charged Porsches. Designed by Tony Southgate, the XJR-6 employed the 'ground effect' principles which had first been seen on the Grand Prix Lotus. To maximise the efficiency of the venturi tunnels which ran along the bottom of the car, helping to keep the car glued to the road, Southgate enclosed the rear wheels in spats (bottom left).*

they finished first and third, with the other car retiring while in second spot. At Mosport, Canada, the XJR-6's made a fine debut. Martin Brundle and Mike Thackwell, who led for the early laps, finished in third place. By then there was little of the season left and the XJR-6's only other success was a second place in the final event at Selangor.

Towards the end of the season Group 44 unveiled a new car, the XJR-7. Aerodynamically improved, it was constructed, like its British cousin, of aluminium and Kevlar. It finished fourth in its first event, the IMSA finale at Daytona Beach; and an XJR-5 driven by Brian Redman and Hurley Haywood failed to take victory by a matter of only eight seconds!

The year 1986 started well. The previous year's sales were again much improved; the company was awarded its third successive Queen's Award to Industry; Derek Warwick and Eddie Cheever took an XJR-6 to victory at Silverstone, beating the factory Rothmans Porsche of Bell and Stuck; and in June the Chairman of the company was knighted.

Three XJR-6's were entered for Le Mans, but not one was to finish. One had fuel pressure problems while lying in fifth place and was stranded out on the circuit. A second car broke a half shaft at 220 mph. The third was in second position after 16 hours' racing when it suffered a puncture at high speed. The flailing rubber did irreparable damage, but even so the car, piloted by Warwick, Cheever and Jean Louis Schlesser, looked magnificent as it went faster and faster during the night.

Sales of the saloons remained strong and demand continued to exceed supply. This happy situation eased the pressure to launch the new XJ40 replacement. It was well known that such a car was coming and Jaguar management had several times postponed its introduction. They were determined that it was going to be absolutely right before it appeared, for the whole future of the company depended upon it. XJ-S sales had picked up well (the Cabriolets were particularly popular), but Jaguar could not survive on them alone.

Styling clinics were set up in Great Britain, the United States and

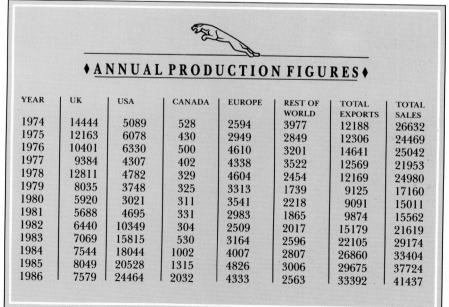

♦ ANNUAL PRODUCTION FIGURES ♦

YEAR	UK	USA	CANADA	EUROPE	REST OF WORLD	TOTAL EXPORTS	TOTAL SALES
1974	14444	5089	528	2594	3977	12188	26632
1975	12163	6078	430	2949	2849	12306	24469
1976	10401	6330	500	4610	3201	14641	25042
1977	9384	4307	402	4338	3522	12569	21953
1978	12811	4782	329	4604	2454	12169	24980
1979	8035	3748	325	3313	1739	9125	17160
1980	5920	3021	311	3541	2218	9091	15011
1981	5688	4695	331	2983	1865	9874	15562
1982	6440	10349	304	2509	2017	15179	21619
1983	7069	15815	530	3164	2596	22105	29174
1984	7544	18044	1002	4007	2807	26860	33404
1985	8049	20528	1315	4826	3006	29675	37724
1986	7579	24464	2032	4333	2563	33392	41437

Germany, Jaguar's three main markets, and acceptability was constantly checked in an effort to take the risk out of the exercise. The hardest car to beat initially was not made by a rival manufacturer – it was the faithful Series III. With refinement of the design, XJ40 took over the number one spot; but the Series III continued to occupy second place.

After Knight's departure, the project came under Jim Randle. A particularly modest man, he took the project from concept to fruition. He began with a very small team which, as fortunes improved, was gradually expanded. In its basic construction the car was similar to Series III, except that it was designed to be made from many fewer panels in order to speed up manufacture, make the car lighter and improve its finish. Convoluted crush tubes allowed the vehicle to pass crash tests in excess of anything required by legislation. Randle and his colleagues also designed a new rear suspension, moving the brakes, which had formerly been mounted inboard, to an outboard position. A unique pendulum arrangement allowed fore and aft movement of the lower wishbone inner fulcrum while still maintaining high lateral stiffness. In this way, very high levels of comfort and road noise isolation were achieved, yet accurate geometric control was maintained for optimum vehicle handling.

■ *ABOVE LEFT In 1986 the TWR Jaguar team acquired sponsorship from Silk Cut and the British racing green livery disappeared as the cars took on the appearance of mobile cigarette packets.*

■ *BELOW LEFT The new XJ40s were tested in crude camouflage panels.*

■ *BELOW Despite retaining skilled craftsmen, Jaguar adopted, wherever possible, all the most modern production aids to increase productivity and quality.*

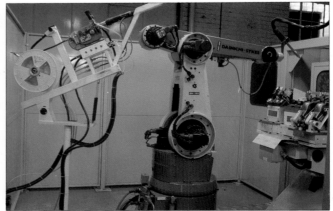

Two versions of the AJ6 engine were fitted in the new car, which inherited its predecessor's name and was known as the XJ6. The 3.6 litre, which had undergone an intensive refining process since its introduction in the XJ-S, was available with the 24-valve head and a 2.9-litre economy version was offered with the May head.

For the new range Jaguar developed an advanced and unique electrical system featuring new types of wiring connectors, up to seven on-board microprocessor control systems and related diagnostic system, plus a new type of wiring known as low-current earth line switching.

An extraordinary amount of testing of the new XJ6's took place, some 5,500,000 miles being covered between early 1982 and the launch in October 1986. This testing was carried out in many countries and several continents, from the gruelling cold of northern Ontario in Canada, where cars had to be capable of withstanding −40 deg C (−105 deg F), to the summer heat of Phoenix, Arizona, where it reaches 50 deg C (122 deg F) at midday.

Other testing included the tough city roads of Manhattan, the dirt roads of the Australian outback, the brutal MIRA pavé track and covering 25,000 miles at near flat-out speeds at the Nardo bowl in southern Italy. A parallel proving programme of component rig testing was also undertaken.

Originally, the V12 engine was intended to die a graceful death, unwanted in this economy age. For this reason, the new car was not designed to accept the larger engine. However, the company changed its mind as demand remained strong for the silky smooth 'twelve'; and when it was discovered that the arch rivals, Mercedes and BMW, were planning such

PROGRAMMED IGNITION

The XJ40's programmed ignition can follow engine requirements with greater precision and flexibility than systems in which the spark is advanced or retarded by a vacuum diaphragm or mechanically. The system is controlled by a microprocessor in response to information relayed by sensors which are able to detect engine load, engine speed, coolant temperature, crankshaft position and throttle opening.

Because it can be programmed with a complex matrix of known engine characteristics, the system provides the flexibility to cater for all engine operating conditions. The major benefit is a smooth and flexible power delivery, even from very low revs when the engine is cold, and an eager but silky response at higher rpm.

The Lucas system fitted to the 3.6-litre engine controls both the fuelling and the ignition. Safeguards are built in to cater for any failures. If there is a loss of air-meter or water-temperature signal, the car will still remain drivable with sufficient power to complete a journey. On the 3.6-engined models, a 'Fuelling Failure' message appears on the vehicle condition monitor screen in the dashboard, while the system reverts to pre-set parameters to maintain reasonable performance.

■ *ABOVE LEFT The XJ40 prototypes were tested in conditions varying from the heat of Arizona to the cold of the Canadian winter, from the dust of the Australian outback to the grind of New York traffic.*

THE JAGUAR DIAGNOSTIC SYSTEM

*H*aving designed the electrical system for the utmost reliability, Jaguar aimed to ensure that the complex task of fault-finding would be made as straightforward and accurate as possible. The Jaguar Diagnostic System is used both on the production line and in Jaguar dealerships worldwide.

It has the ability, first, not to interfere with or change electronic functions during the diagnostic process and, second, to examine components and circuitry under vehicle operating conditions. The electrical current probe is a 'non-intrusive' device (to use the modern jargon) which can measure the currents flowing through components such as relay-coils, motors and lamps. The measurement probe can simulate certain switched functions and take voltage measurements. In plain terms, it should make maintenance and repairs more of a science and, by making them easier for the garage, quicker and cheaper for the customer.

What happens to subsequent owners of today's ultra-sophisticated cars who cannot afford, or are unable to take their car to, a Jaguar dealer equipped with JDS is anybody's guess!

■ *RIGHT Benefiting from experience on the race tracks, TWR introduced its version of the XJ-S, with the addition of body-styling panels and modifications to the engine, suspension and braking.*

◆ JAGUAR ◆
XJ6 SOVEREIGN &
DAIMLER (XJ40)

BODY STYLE(s): Large Saloon
ENGINE: AJ6 2919 cc AJ6 24 valve 3590 cc
MAX POWER: 165 bhp & 221 bhp
TIME: 0–60   9.6 secs (2.9 XJ6)
7.4 secs (3.6 XJ6) 10.8 secs (2.9
Sovereign)
8.8 secs (3.6 Sovereign & Daimler)
MAX SPEED: 120 mph (2.9 XJ6)
136 mph (3.6 XJ6)
118 mph (2.9 Sovereign)
135 mph (3.6 Sovereign & Daimler)
QUANTITY MADE: Still in production
PRICE: £16,495 (2.9 XJ6)
£18,495 (3.6 XJ6)
£22,995 (2.9 Sovereign)
£24,995 (3.6 Sovereign)
£28,495 (Daimler)
ANNOUNCEMENT DATE: Oct 1986
IN PRODUCTION: 1987 –

■ *The new XJ40, confusingly named the XJ6, finally arrived in late 1986 with a top-of-the-range Daimler model (｜LEFT); with the AJ6 engine and a dashboard bristling with electronics (BELOW) and, on automatic versions, the 'J gate' selector (BOTTOM).*

engines there was no question. It was not possible for the necessary redesign to be carried out in time for the V12 version to be launched with the other versions and so the Series III HE will continue in production for a while until a stretched V12-engined XJ40 appears, probably in 1988.

The reception that the new XJ6, the more up-market Sovereign and the top-of-the-range Daimler received was reminiscent of reaction reserved for Sir William's launches. The problem was to manufacture enough to meet demand within a reasonable time. Within weeks, the waiting list in Great Britain was over a year. The launch in the United States in May went well, with the new models receiving wide acceptance and praise. Jaguar once more had a name for style, speed, refinement and, above all, quality.

There are exciting new models in the pipeline. A sports car is due in the early nineties and updates are planned for the XJ-S (a full convertible introduced in 1988) and for the Saloons. Families of cars are to be developed from each basic model to give a good spread once more – and the greater security that goes with it. Jaguar is once again a splendid example of British engineering, blended with traditional craftsmanship, at its very best.

As for the racing, Derek Warwick had the misfortune of failing to take the 1986 Drivers' Championship by a single point. For 1987, he decided to concentrate on Formula One racing. Eddie Cheever remained to lead the Silk Cut TWR team and was paired with Brazilian Raul Boesel. The second car was to be driven by the Dutchman, Jan Lammers, and the immensely experienced and popular John Watson. The Danish driver, John Nielson, was to deputize for Cheever when Grand Prix dates clashed with sports car events.

The season started superbly for the revised and renamed XJR-8 cars. Some 60 changes had been made under the skin and the engines had been enlarged to 7 litres, producing some 700 horsepower. Watson and Lammers took first place at the season's opener at Jarama, with Cheever and Boesel third. A week later at Jerez, also in Spain, it was Cheever's turn to win. Watson and Lammers won at Monza and at Silverstone the TWR Jaguars took first and second positions, Cheever and Boesel leading their colleagues home.

■ BELOW, BELOW LEFT AND BOTTOM RIGHT *Outright success eluded Jaguar at Le Mans in 1987; the one car that finished spent a considerable time in the pits having its gearbox rebuilt: parts were cannibalized from the spare built-up unit.*

■ LEFT *The Jaguar team had the satisfaction of winning a number of rounds other than Le Mans, including Silverstone. They subsequently annexed the Manufacturers' Championship, with Boesel taking the Drivers' Championship.*

XJR-8, SPRINT

XJR-8LM, LE MANS

■ *ABOVE For 1987, Southgate designed the XJR-8, and an additional XJR-8LM model with revised bodywork adapted specifically for the Le Mans race and its fast 3½-mile Mulsanne straight.*

This unblemished record made the Jaguars the favourites to win Le Mans. But, despite adding a third car, driven by Nielsen and Martin Brundle, it was not to be. The three Le Mans Jaguars were, in fact, rather different cars from those that had raced in the earlier events; subtle, but important, aerodynamic changes were made to suit the French circuit. After a variety of problems two of the cars retired and the third, having spent a long period in the pits, eventually finished fifth. The result was a great disappointment, especially as all three cars had occupied the top three positions, and the Jaguars had led for a good proportion of the race.

In April the company received the Queen's award for Technological Achievement for designing and developing the new XJ6s and the influential German magazine, *Auto Motor und Sport*, voted the XJ6 the best imported luxury car (the V12 Daimler Double Six was given second place).

In May it was announced that the running of the American team would no longer be entrusted to Group 44, but would be taken on by TWR from a new American base. Back in Europe, the team regained its winning form, taking first and third places at Brands Hatch, a result which virtually sowed up the Manufacturers' Championship for Jaguar and took Boesel into the lead for the Drivers' Championship, which he duly won. The new US team began 1988 well with first and third places at Daytona.

Jaguar celebrated 60 years of car manufacturing on 20 May 1987. Sales and production records have been continually broken, and it is clear that the company faces the future in a spirit of well-founded optimism.

■ The changing face of the company's products as shown by the evolution of radiators and later grilles: TOP, LEFT TO RIGHT *Standard Swallow, Wolseley Hornet Swallow and pre-war 1½-litre Saloon.* ABOVE LEFT *SS Jaguar 100.* ABOVE *post-war Jaguar 1½-litre Saloon.* FAR LEFT *post-war Jaguar 3½-litre Saloon.* LEFT *Jaguar XK120.*

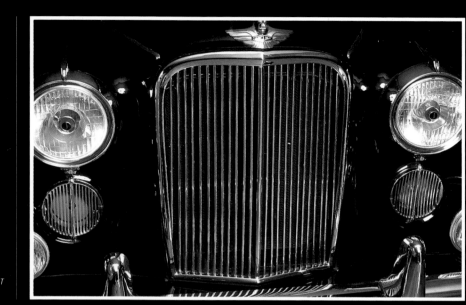

■ RIGHT *Jaguar Mark IX Saloon.* BELOW *Jaguar Mark II Saloon.* BELOW RIGHT *Jaguar XK140.* BOTTOM LEFT *Jaguar S-type Saloon.* BOTTOM RIGHT *Jaguar Mark X Saloon.*

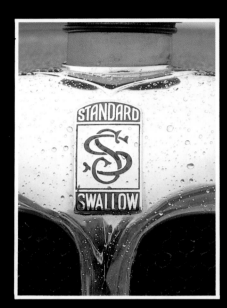

■ *A closer look at the badges that appeared atop the radiators and grilles:* TOP, LEFT TO RIGHT *Austin Seven Swallow Saloon, Standard Swallow and Wolseley Hornet Swallow.* LEFT *SS Jaguar Saloon.* BELOW LEFT *SS Jaguar 100.* BELOW *post-war Jaguar 1½-litre Saloon.*

ABOVE Jaguar 3½-litre Saloon. ABOVE RIGHT Jaguar XK120. RIGHT Jaguar XK140. BELOW Jaguar Mark II Saloon. BELOW RIGHT Jaguar S-type Saloon.

INDEX

Page references in *italic* refer to captions.

Adams, Ronnie, 81, 96
advertising, *15, 17, 19, 24, 28, 34*, 35, *42*, 64, *64*, 66, *90–1, 128*, 133, *174*, 198
aircraft construction, 44
AJ6 engine, 179, 204, *204*, 213
all-steel saloons, 37, *42*
Alpine Rally:
    1948, 40, *45*
    1950, 67
    1951, 71
Alpine Trial:
    1936, 36
aluminium bodies, 66, 148, 150, 153, 155
aluminium engines, 204
Appleyard, Ian, 40, *45*, 66, 67, 71, *72*, 81, 95, 96
Atkins, Tommy, 157
Austin, *Sir* Herbert, 16
Austin Swallow
    saloon, 14–15, *14–15*
    two-seater, *9*, 10–11, *12–13*, 14–15
automatic transmission, 94, 97, 155, 164, 172

Badges, identification of, 220–21
Baillie, *Sir* Gawaine, 101
Baily, Claude, 49, 58, 161
Beasley, Mike, 199
Berry, Bob, 35, 148
Bertone, 84
Bigger, Frank, 97
Biondetti, Clemente, 66, 124
Bira, *Prince*, 64
Birmingham plant, 10, 13, *192*, 198
Black, *Sir* John, 47
Blackpool, 10, 12, 13
BMC, 163, 176–7
Boesel, Raul, 217
Borg and Beck clutches, 129
Bowman's Garage, 97
Brabham, Jack, 114, 152
braking systems, 79, 84, 94, 99, 122, 126, 135, 150, 158, 180
Brands Hatch, 111
    1984, 208
    1985, *211*
    1987, 217
British Leyland, 17, 114, 124, 177, 182, 188, 190, 192–3, 199–200, 208
British Motor Corporation *see* BMC
British Motor Holdings, 177
British Touring Car Championship:
    1958, 101
Brookes, Ted, *142*
Brooklands competitions, 44
    1937, 36
Brown, Eric, 35
Brown and Mallalieu, 10, 11
Brundle, Martin, 211, 217
B-type head, 80, 82, 97, 98, 103
Bueb, Ivor, 98, 137, 139, 141

Campbell, Donald, *83*
carburettors, 82, *91*, 98, 126, 164, 178
C/D Jaguar, 148
Chapman, Colin, 106
Cheever, Eddie, 211, 217
Clark, Jim, 114
colour schemes, 14–15, *54*
competitive events, 22, 36, 40, *72*, 81, 94–5
concours d'élégance, 22
Consten, Bernard, 106
Coombs, John, 106, 152–3, 157

Coupe des Alpes, 40, 67
Coventry Climax Company, 114, 161, 184
Coventry plant, 10, 13–14, 52, 104, 114, *192*
Crossley Motors, 10
Crystal Palace track, 153
C-type head, 58
C-type Jaguar, 33, 122, *123, 125*, 126, *127–8,* 129, *130–1,* 132–3, 142
Cunningham, Briggs, 141, 152, 153, 156–7, *158*

Daimler Company, 104, 172
Daimler Double Six, *191, 217*
Daimler Limousine, 178–9, *178*
Daimler Sovereign, *177*
Danny, Robert, 169
Dawtrey, Clifford, 37
Daytona Beach track, 211
Williams Deacon's Bank, 10, 12
design *see* styling
Dewis, Norman, 71, 142, 162
diagnostics, 214
distribution, 11, 13, *15, 24*, 40
diversification, 44, 47, 114, 161, 172
Dobson, Bill, 142
D-type Jaguar, 33, 78, 84, *121,* 133, *133,* 135–6, *135–40,* 138–9, 141–2, *142,* 148
Dunlop tyres, 79, 135, 180, 203
Dykestra, Lee, 204

Earls Court *see* Motor Show
Ecurie Ecosse, *140,* 141–2
Edwardes, *Sir* Michael, 192, 193, 198, 199
Egan, *Sir* John, 17, 198–200, 206, 208, 211
England, 'Lofty', 49, 64, 124, *130,* 186, 188, 199
Ensign *see* Standard Ensign Swallow
Equipe Endeavour, 152
E-type Jaguar, 33, 109, 133, 135, *142,* 145–69, *145–6, 148–51, 153, 155–9,* 161–2, 194
    2+2, 155, *155,* 158, *159, 161,* 164, 166, *167–9*
    4.2, 153
    E1A, 148
    E2A, 152
    Fixed head coupe, 149, *149,* 152, 153–4, 157, 164, *167,* 169
    lightweight, 153, 155–7, *156–7, 159*
    Roadster, 150, 152, 153–4, 157, 158, 164, 166, *167, 169*
    Series II, 155, 157–8, *161*
    Series III, 164, *164–5,* 166, *167–9*
European Touring Car Championship, 203
    1963, 112
    1984, 206
PJ Evans Ltd, 11, 169
exports, 10, 17, 28, 49, *54,* 62, 66, *88,* 94, 163, 194, 203, 211–12
    see also distribution

Fairman, Jack, 66, 124, *125, 130,* 139, 148
Fangio, Ivan Manuel, *137,* 138
Charles Faroux Team Trophy, 96
Fenton, Alice, 23
FIAT Swallow, 16
Fielden, David, 192
Fleetwing chassis, 16
Flockhart, Ron, 142

Foleshill plant, *47*
Frankfurt Motor Show, 186
Frere, Paul, 139
Frey, Emil, 10, 17
Frey, Walter, 17
fuel injection, 164, 166, 194, 208

Gardner, Gordon, 128
gearing, 82, 95, 135, 153, 172, 194, 204
    see also automatic transmission
Geneva Motor Show, 148
Getrag gearbox, 204
Ghia, 84
Girling brakes, 94, 158, 180
Giron, Louis, 97
Goodwood track, 155
Grilles, identification of, *218–19*
Grinham, Edward, 37
Grossman, Bob, 156, 157
Group 44, 166, *169,* 194, 201, *202,* 203–4, 206, *206,* 208, 211, 217
Gurney, Dan, 110, 152
Guy Motors, 114

Haddon, Eric, 81
Hadley, HL, 66
Haines, Nick, 66
Hamilton, Duncan, 97, 98, 101, 127, 129, *131, 135,* 136
Hansgen, Walt, 101, 141, 152, 157
James Hardie 1000:
    1984, 208, 211
Harriman, *Sir* George, 177
Harrop, Jack, 36
Hassan, Wally, 44, 47, 58, 64, 96, 114, 161, 182–6
Hastings, Harold, 122
Hawthorn, Mike, 97, 98, 101, 129, *137,* 138–9, 141
Haywood, Hurley, 211
HE engine, 199–200
Henly, Bertie, 11
Henly's, 11, 13, *15, 24, 42*
Heyer, Hans, *211*
Heynes, William, 11, 32–3, *34,* 37, 49, *50,* 58, 60, 66, 96, 122, *123,* 148, 158, 161–2, *162,* 178, 182, 184, 193
Hill, Graham, *103,* 106, 110, 111, 152–3, 155, 157, *157*
Hill, Phil, *64,* 67
Hobbs David, 81, 162
Hornet *see* Wolseley Hornet
Hough, Frank, 11
Huffaker Engineering, 166
Humber cars, 37

Indianapolis track, 206, 208
International Alpine Trial:
    1933, 22
Issigonis, *Sir* Alec, 96

Jabbeke track, 64, 71
Jacob, EH, 36
Jaguar cars
    420G, 176–7, *177*
    C/D, 148
    C-type, 33, 122, *123, 125,* 126, *127–8,* 129, *130–1,* 132–3, 142
    D-type, 33, 78, 84, *121,* 133, *133,* 135–6, *135–40,* 138–9, 141–2, *142,* 148
    E-type, 33, 109, 133, 135, *142,* 145–69, *146, 148–51, 153, 155–9,* 161–2, 194
    Mark II series, 102–3, *103, 105–6,* 106, *108,* 110–12, 115, *115,* 172, *178*
    Mark IV series, 88

Mark V series, 49, 50–3, 52, 54, *54*, 59, 62
Mark VII series, 88, *88–95*, 94–7
Mark VIII series, 97–9, *97, 99*
Mark IX series, 99–101, *100*, 103
Mark X series, 106, 109–12, *111, 113, 116*, 172, *173–5*, 176–7
Special Equipment models, 58
SS series, 16, *17*, 18–27, *18–25, 27, 29*, 35, *35, 36, 42*
S-type, 112, 115, *116*, 117, *118–19*, 176
XF, 58–9
XJ series, 59, *171*, 172–215, *174–5, 177–8, 180, 182–3, 185–8, 191–2, 195, 200, 202–4, 208, 211–13*, 217
XK series, 33, 58–85, *59, 62–84*
see also Daimler
Jaguar Cars Ltd, 49–177
see also SS Cars
Jaguar Drivers' Club, 35
Jaguar SS100 *see* SS100
Jane, Bob, 157
Jarama, 217
Jerez, 217
Johnston, Frank, 97
Jones, Alan, 208, *211*
Jones, Tom, 148, 178

Kelsy, 111
Knight, Bob, 11, 96, 110, 122, 148, 178, 183, 190–3, 198–9, 212

Lambert, Jack, 81
Lammers, Jan, 208, *211*, 217
Le Mans, 81, 122, 126, 128, 135, 138, 148, 152, 177, 204
  1950, 66–7
  1951, 122, *123*, 124
  1952, 125
  1953, 126, *130–1*, 132–3
  1954, 135–6, *135*
  1955, *137*, 138
  1956, *140*, 142
  1957, 139, *140*, 141–2
  1962, 153
  1963, 156, *159*
  1984, *202*, 206
  1986, 211
  1987, 217
Leslie, Ed, 157
Levegh, Pierre, 125
Liège-Rome-Liège Rally:
  1951, 71
lightweight E-type, 153, 155–7, *156–7*, 159
Lindner, Peter, 106, 112, 157
Lister-Jaguars, 141
LNW 100, 40, *45*
Loewy, Raymond, 84
Lucas-Bosch fuel injection, 208
Lumsden, Peter, 157
Lynx Engineering, 204
Lyons, *Sir* William, 10–11, 17, 18, *20*, 22–3, 37, 40, 44, 49, 84, 94, 114, 172, 180
  and Sir William Black, 47, 49
  and BMC, 176–7
  and British Leyland, 177, 1206
  and Lofty England, 124
  and Bill Heynes, 32, 33, 37
  and motor racing, 122, *123, 130*, 132, 148, 169
  and Bill Rankin, 35
  and William Walmsley, 16, 26
  and XK series, 58, 62, 66
  knighthood, 79
  retirement, 124, 186, 199

Mark II series, 102–3, *103, 105–6*, 106, *108*, 110–12, 115, *115*, 172, *178*
Mark IV series, 88
Mark V series, 49, *50–3*, 52, 54, *54*, 59, 62
  Drophead, 52, 54, *54*
  Saloon, *48–9*, 52, *52*
Mark VII series, 88, *88–95*, 94–7
  VII M, 94, 95
  Saloon, 95–6, *96*
Mark VIII series, 97–9, *97, 99*
Mark IX series, 99–101, *100*, 103
Mark X series, 106, 109–12, *111, 113*, 115–16, *116*, 172, *173–5*, 176–7
Marne Sports Car Grand Prix:
  1936, 36
mascots, 98
May, Michael, 198, 204
May Fireball combustion chamber, 198–9
McLaren, Bruce, 106, 156, 157
Henry Meadows Ltd, 114
microprocessor control systems, 213
Mille Miglia, 126
  1950, 66
Monte Carlo Rally, *94*
  1952, 94
  1953, 95
  1955, 96–7
  1956, 97
  1959, 101
Montlhery track, 66
Monza, 217
Morecambe Rally:
  1951, 71
Morrill, Frank, 157
Morris Cowley Swallow, 11, 13, *13*
Mosport track, 211
Moss, Stirling, 66, 67, 71, 95, 106, 124, 125, *125*, 129, *131*, 136, 138
Motor Panels Ltd, 47
Motor Show:
  1931, 18
  1932, 18
  1948, 41
  1950, *88*, 94
  1961, 106
motorcycles, 10, *11*, 17, 47
Mundy, Harry, 161, 186
Murray, David, 142

nationalization, 188, 190
Nelson Advertising Agency, 35
Newsome, Sammy, 36, 84
Nielson, John, 217
Nocker, Peter, 112, 157
NUB 120, *72*
Nürburgring:
  1961, 106

Old No. 8, 36, *41*
Oulton Park track, 152–3

Panhard rod mountings, 98
Parker, Don, 81
Parkers, 10, 11
Parkes, Mike, 106, 110, 155
Parks, Bobbie, 81
Pearce, Warren, 81
Pebble Beach Cup Race:
  1950, 67
performance, 18, 32, 36, 37, 62
Pininfarina, 84, 192
Pop Rivet Special, 149–50
Potter, 40

power steering, 164, 172
premises, 10, 12, 13–14, *47*, 52, 78, 94, 104, 172, *192*
Pressed Steel, 37
privatization, 203, 208
production levels, 14, 16, 22, 26, 49, 72, 77, 94, 150, 166, 188, 198, 203, 211
Production Touring Car Race:
  1952, 95
  1953, 95
  1954, 95
programmed ignition, 213
publicity *see* advertising

Queen's Award to Industry, 206, 211
Queen's Award for Technological Achievement, 217
Qvale, Kjell, 157

racing cars:
  C/D, 148
  C-type, 33, 122, *123, 125*, 126, 127–8, 129, *130–1*, 132–3, 142
  D-type, 33, 78, 84, 133, *133*, 135–6, *135–40*, 138–9, 141–2, *142*, 148
  E-type, 33, 109, 133, 135, *142*, 145–69, *146, 148–51, 153, 155–9*, 161–2, 194
  XJ13, 33, 135, 162, *162*
  XK series, 33, 58–85, *59, 62–84*
Radford plant, 172
Rainbow, Frank, 66
rallies *see* competitive events
Rallye Soleil:
  1951, 71
Randle, Jim, 212
Rankin, Ernest 'Bill', 35
rationalization, 115, 172
Redman, Brian, 157, 211
Rheims track, *135*, 142
Richards, 157
Robinson, Geoffrey, 188, 190
Rodway, Stanley, 11
Rolt, Tony, 95, *127*, 129, *131*, 135–6, *136*
Rubery Owen, 47
Ryder Report, 188, 190, 192

sales *see* distribution exports
saloon cars
  420G, 176–7, *177*
  Austin Swallow, 14–15, *14–15*
  Daimler Double Six, 191, 217
  Daimler Limousine, 189–9, *178*
  Daimler Sovereign, 177
  Mark II series, 102–3, *103, 105–6*, 106, *108*, 110–12, 115, *115*, 172, *178*
  Mark IV series, 88
  Mark V series, 49, *50–3*, 52, 54, *54*, 59, 62
  Mark VII series, 88, *88–95*, 94–7
  Mark VIII series, 97–9, *97, 99*
  Mark IX series, 99–101, *100*, 103
  Mark X series, 106, 109–12, *113, 115–16*, 172, *173–5*, 176–7
  SS series, 16, *16*, 18–27, *18–25, 27, 29*, 35, *35, 36, 42*
  S-type, 112, 115, *116*, 117, *118–19*, 176
  XJ series, 59, 172–215, *174–5, 177–8, 180, 182–3, 185–8, 191–2, 195, 200, 202–4, 208, 211–13*
Salvadori, Roy, 101, *103*, 106, 111, 152–3, 156, 157
Sanderson, Ninian, 142
Sargent, Peter, 157
Sayer, Malcolm, 33, 122, 135, 148, 162, *162*
SCCA C-Production Championship: 1955, 81

SCCS National Championship:
  1975, 166
Schlesser, Jean Louis, 211
Scott, Denis, 95
Scott-Brown, Archie, 141
Scott-Douglas, *Sir* James, 142
Scragg, Phil, 157
Sears, Jack, 106, 110, 111, 157
Selangor track, 211
Shell Oil, 66
Shelsley Walsh hillclimb:
  1936, 36, *41*
  1937, 36
  1938, 41
  1950, 67
sidecars, 10–11, *11*, 14, 41, 44, 49
Silk Cut, *212*
Silverstone Grand Prix:
  1949, 64, *71*
  1950, 67, *71*
  1951, 71
  1986, 211
  1987, 217
Silverstone Saloon Car Race:
  1955, 97
  1956, 97
Silverstone Touring Car Race:
  1957, 98
Simms, Frederick Richard, 104
Smith, Don, 81
Solex carburettors, 178
Sopwith, Tommy, 101
Southgate, Tony, 206, *211*
Special Equipment models
  XK120, 58
  XK140, 75
  XK150, 80
specials, 84, 149–50
SS100, 36, *36–41*, 40, 45, *45–6*
  LNW 100, 40, *45*
  Old No. 8, 36, *41*
SS Cars, 11, 26–49
  see also Jaguar Cars Ltd
  Swallow Sidecar Company
SS series, 16, *16*, 18–27, *18–21*, *23–5*, 27, *29*, *35*, *42*
  SS1, 18, *18–19*, *21*, 22, *23–5*, 26, 32, 36
  SS1 Airline, 22, 27
  SS1 Coupe, *20–1*, *25*
  SS1 Drophead, 26, 28, *29*
  SS1 Saloon, 22, *24*
  SS1 Tourers, 22, *22*, *29*, 35, *35*
  SSII, *20*, 22, *25*, 27
  SSII Coupe, *22*, *25*
  SSII Saloon, *25*
  SSII Tourer, *25*
  SS90, 26, 29, 36
Standard Ensign Swallow, 16
Standard Little Nine, 18, *20*
Standard Motor Company, 16, *16*, 18, 32, 33, 35, 37, 47, 52, 58, 59
Standard Swallow, 16
Steely, Norman, 11
steering, 75, 164, 180
Stewart, Ian, 142
Stewart, Jackie, 157
Stewart, Jimmy, 97, 129, 142
Stokes, *Lord*, 177, 188
styling, 84, 97–8, 102, 109–10, 122, 133, 135, 148, 153, 155, 158, 201, 203, 206, 211–13
S-type head, 82, 84
S-type Jaguar, 112, 115, *116*, 117, *118–19*, 176
SU carburettors, 82, 98
Suez crisis, 97

Surtees, John, 106
suspension, 96, 109, 112, 122, 129, 135, 148, 150, 162, 180, 212
Sutcliffe, Peter, 157
Sutton, Joe, 128
Sutton, 'Soapy', 64
Swallow Coachbuilding (1935) Ltd, 44
Swallow Sidecar Company, 10–26
  see also SS Cars
Swallow Swift, 16

Tanzola, Warren 'Tanz', 75
Taylor, Bob, 36
Teather, Constance, 23
Teather, Harry, 23
Thackwell, Mike, 211
Titterington, Desmond, 97
Tour de France, 115
  1951, 71
  1961, 106
Tourist Trophy:
  1950, 67
  1951, 125
  1982, 203
trading profits, 108
Trans-Am competition, 201
transmission systems *see* gearing
Tulip Rally:
  1951, 71
  1952, 95
  1953, 95
  1958, 101
  1960, 81
Tullius, Bob, 166, 194
twin carburettors, *91*
TWR *see* Tom Walkinshaw Racing

United States, *64–5*, 72, 75–6, 81, 152, 158, *161*, 166, 172, *202*, 215
  see also exports

V8 Chrysler engines, 75, 82, 146
V12 engines, 158, 161–2, 164, *164*, 180, 183–4, 191–2, 198, 200, 208, 213
  HE, 204, *204*, 215, 217
V12E *see* E-type Jaguar, Series III
VA vehicle, 47
Vard, Cecil, 96
VB vehicle, 47
vibration, 204
Vivien, Charles, 81

Walker, Peter, 64, 66, 67, *71*, 124, *125*, 129, *130–1*
Tom Walkinshaw Racing, 203, 206, *206*, 208, 210, *212*, *214*, 217
Wallace, Chuck, 81
Walmsley, William, 10, 16, 26
Warwick, Derek, 211, 217
Watkins Glen Grand Prix:
  1951, 71
Watson, John, 217
Weaver, Phil, 148
Weber carburettors, 126
Welsh Rally:
  1937, 36
Weslake, Harry, 26, 32, *34*, 37, 58, 82
Wharton, Ken, 97, *135*, 136
Whitehead, Peter, 125, *125*, 129, *130–1*, *135*, 136
Whittaker, Arthur, 10, 11, 23, 32, 182
Wilkins, Dick, 157
Wilkinson, Wilkie, 142
Wisdom, Bill, 36, *41*
Wisdom, Elsie, 36, *41*
Wisdom, Tommy, 66, 67

Wolseley Hornet Special, 16
Wolseley Hornet Swallow, 16, *17*
World Championship of Makes, 194
World War II, 41, 44, 47, 58, 104, 114

XA 58
XF 58–9
XG 59
XJ Series, 59, *171*, 172–215
  Coupes, 188, 191, *191*
  Series II, 186–8, *188*
  Series III, 192–4, 195, *200*, 212, 215
  XJ6, 176–7, 178, 180, *180*, 181–3, *182–3*, *184*, 189, 191, *197*, 213, 215, 217
  XJ12, 184–6, *184*, *186*, 189
  XJ12 HE, 199
  XJ40, 192, *200*, 212, *212–13*, 215
  XJR-5, 208
  XJR-6, 206, 208, *208*, 211, *211*
  XJR-7, 211
  XJR-8, 217
  XJ-S, 191–2, *195*, 200, *202*, 203–4, *206*, 208, *208*, *214*, 215
  XJ-SC, 204–6
  XJ-SCHE, 104
  XJ-SHE, 104
XJ4 project, 178
XK 120C *see* C-type Jaguar
XK engines, 60, 88, 91, 94, 95, 96, 109, 122, *139*, 141, 153, *155*, *164*, *173*, 178, 180, 204
XK Series, 33, 58–85, *59*, *62–84*
  XK100, 62
  XK120, *57*, 58, 59–64, *59*, *64–73*, 66–7, 71–2, 122, *131*, 142, 146
  XK120 Drophead Coupe, 71–2, *72*
  XK120 Fixed Head Coupe, 64, 66, *67*
  XK120M, 58
  XK120 Roadster, 62–3, *63*
  XK140, 72, *74–5*, 75–7, 79, *80*
  XK140 Drophead Coupe, *74*, 75–7
  XK140 Roadster, *76*
  XK150, 79–82, 84
  XK150 Drophead Coupe, 82
  XK150 Fixed Head Coupe, *81*, 82, *83*
  XK150 Roadster, *81*, 82, *83*
  XK150S, 82, 83
  XKSS, 79–9, *78–9*, 148
XK-E *see* E-type Jaguar

Zenith carburettors, 164
ZF gearboxes, 155, 162

31